SOUL SEARCHING

Edited by

Heather Killingray

First published in Great Britain in 1999 by
POETRY NOW
Remus House,
Coltsfoot Drive,
Woodston,
Peterborough, PE2 9JX
Telephone (01733) 898101
Fax (01733) 313524

Copyright Contributors 1999

HB ISBN 0 75430 747 6
SB ISBN 0 75430 748 4

FOREWORD

Although we are a nation of poets we are accused of not reading poetry, or buying poetry books. After many years of listening to the incessant gripes of poetry publishers, I can only assume that the books they publish, in general, are books that most people do not want to read.

Poetry should not be obscure, introverted, and as cryptic as a crossword puzzle: it is the poet's duty to reach out and embrace the world.

The world owes the poet nothing and we should not be expected to dig and delve into a rambling discourse searching for some inner meaning.

The reason we write poetry (and almost all of us do) is because we want to communicate: an ideal; an idea; or a specific feeling. Poetry is as essential in communication, as a letter; a radio; a telephone, and the main criteria for selecting the poems in this anthology is very simple: they communicate.

CONTENTS

THESE POEMS OF MINE

Sometimes at night when I lie in my bed,
With all sorts of things going round in my head,
A poem comes to mind, and I scribble away,
Trying to think of the right things to say.

Sometimes they're silly, and sometimes they're sad,
Sometimes they're good, and quite often they're bad!
        These poems of mine!

I've written of fairies, of cats and of life.
I've written of sadness, of memories and strife!
Of family and spaceships, of war, and of smiles,
I've scribbled away for miles and for miles!
        These poems of mine!

I'd love to be famous, to get my poems seen,
And maybe have a few of them read by the Queen!
But . . . until that day comes, I'll just have to contend,
With reading my poetry to family and friend!
        These poems of mine!

Sylvia E L Reynolds

AUTUMN

Autumn is a time when summer blooms
are fading into golden days.
With sunlight falling on golden leaves,
creating a beauty for all to perceive.
It's just like life, as we grow old
our beauty is deep within our souls.
We now take time to look
for the beauty in every season,
as it creates something new.

Sandra McKinnon

SECOND'S GLANCE

I look into her eyes
To see the love that shines
For another man
That she only can
She looks into my eyes
And sees the love that hides
Deep inside my soul
Watching as it grows
I look upon her face
Feel my heartbeat race
Trembling with the fear
From the faint drip tears
She looks upon my face
Blank expression smile in haste
The love for her she doesn't see
That of which belongs to me.

Graham Hagger

GONE SO QUICK

I know you are all saddened by her sudden death,
maybe speechless and feeling numb.
But right now, maybe even this very minute,
she's up there being greeted by her mum.
And I can only imagine the emptiness
that you all, right now, must feel.
And only by what I have been told,
that it will take a while to heal.
For Angela not to have suffered long,
we all know for her to go quickly was best.
For now she's sleeping peacefully in heaven,
now that you have all laid her down to rest.

D Stopher

HE'S LOOKING OLD

How wrinkled is his furrowed brow
He's looking old, I've noticed now,
Yet underneath still I can see
The younger man he used to be.
Spectacles have taken place
A new expression on his face,
And as he peers beyond their gaze
I know he dreams of childhood days.
His hair now bears first signs of grey
He wishes they would go away,
Whilst posture once so proud and tall
Is slightly crouched, he seems now small.
Ancient scars upon each hand
Through years of toil upon the land,
With fingers stained by nicotine
From grasping roll-ups in between.
He walks now at a leisured gait
A walking stick to keep him straight,
And stops awhile to ease his chest
After several steps he needs to rest.
A lonely man, most friends have gone
He knows for sure it won't be long,
Before his life will be no more
And death will tap upon his door.

Maria Colvin

THE CREATURES

In the land of Long Shadows, the creatures they hide
Behind the tall stories and the little white lies
And the sun never rises, for the sun never sets
And in the Temple of Memories, the righteous never forget.

John C Farman

STUDENT DAYS

You bring a child into the world and from that very day
She filled your life with love and joy in her own special way

She made you laugh, she made you cry, she brought you
so much pleasure
The special days you all have shared, such memories to treasure

You watched her grow and time went by, the years they passed so fast
Those early days, the teenage times, it's all now in the past

But take pride in her achievements, of what she has become
You made her what she is today and so your job is done

And now the time has come at last a new life she will start
So kiss your child and let her go this is the hardest part

Her student life beginning, an endless social whirl
And even tho' she's all grown up, she'll always be your girl

Yet I know to part is painful, and your heart is torn in two
But wipe your tears and wish her well, she's off to pastures new

And tho' it seems you've lost her and you're many miles apart
She'll never really leave you, she's right there in your heart.

Stephanie Bines

TWIRL

I would like shoes of gold, or silver
To set me on my feet,
A dancer, swathed in scarlet,
But this is life's receipt;
A heavy heart and a dead weight,
The desire to be gone,
Fitting wages for a fall from grace,
Soles of lead to put on.

Still I dream that silver shoes, or gold
One day may grace my feet,
A dancer, clothed in pure white,
For this is love's receipt;
A new start and a clean slate,
Redemption dearly won,
A new heart and a new face,
A new Earth to dance upon.

Andria J Cooke

LOVELESSNESS IS INSTITUTIONALISED

Lovelessness is institutionalised,
From the day I was born, to the day I die.

You see people being unloved,
But that ain't me,
I got too much to give,
Too much love in me.

I think I must have someone else's,
I seem to care too much,
Sometimes I want to be unloving,
But I don't got the guts.

I should be glad,
'Coz of what I can do,
I can be kind to all,
And kind to you.

But it's also a burden,
A burden on my back,
Sometimes it gets to me,
I feel too much empathy,
Like a pain striking through me,
Lovelessness is institutionalised.

Nate Chapman (16)

THE LINE DANCER'S RAP

Here we go then, step, heel, toe,
All in line now, here we go,
Step to the side and bend those knees,
Turn to the left - smile now please.

Listen to the music, sway those hips,
Be flamboyant, pout those lips,
Turn to the left then step, heel, toe,
Raise those Stetsons, don't let go!

Raise those arms and whoop with glee,
One more time now, turn to me,
Whip those skirts up, front to back,
Turn to your partner, Jill to Jack.

Keep repeating one, two, three,
All twist round now then face me.
On we'll dance 'til the night is done,
All dressed up and having fun!

Alice Ackland

THE VEIL OF NIGHT

Incongruous night has sealed the lips of departing day
But not yet touched the brow of dawn to be.
Its spell of gloom is cast, its darkened hours begun,
When fears of men are magnified, as shadows grow in dying light.
Then time slows down its turning wheels for those who sleepless lie,
Their hapless state the ready prey for morbid thoughts,
The loveless ones who feel no touch of human warmth
And only wait for dawn to come,
The birth of hope and yet another day.

Bernard Wright

BOTTLES

Man's troubled passage through this life is marked by different stages,
Which Shakespeare aptly specified as Mankind's Seven Ages.
What he might have noticed too, as through each stage we pass,
Is how each age depends upon containers made of glass.
When first he's snatched from Mother's breast, how does the babe
survive?
Without a bottle filled with milk, he'd not long stay alive.
When with his shining morning face, to school he makes his way,
It's bottles full of Coke he needs to see him through the day.
When he aspires to manhood, he seeks out stronger stuff,
As with a lager lining he feels handsome, lean and tough.
If he survives that dangerous age, and learns to hold his drink,
And bottles do not land him up in graveyard or in clink,
He feels immune, and very soon invites a girl to dine,
And fails to see what perils lurk in after-dinner wine;
A bottle shared in candlelight at a table near the band,
Till, with his judgement blurred by wine, he asks her for her hand.
Next in the church he takes the oath, his loved one by his side,
Renouncing youthful, carefree ways, to serve his precious bride.
Are bottles banished from his life? Plainly they are not,
For it's bottles full of best champagne that seal the nuptial knot.
In middle days, again he strays, though perhaps not to the pub,
For it's rounds of golf and business talks, scotch and soda at the Club.
Then, sadly, comes the final age, but sans bottle? Not at all!
The bottle rules his life until he hears the Final Call.
That bottle-need that dogged his path, in dotage gets much worse,
As from his sickbed comes the cry: 'Quick, bring a bottle, nurse!'

Norman Ford

THE POET

For what reason were they born this night?
So unsure of their place, their meaning.
They stand in groups around the table light,
Brought to life by poet's dreaming.

Small footprints lead where fairies be,
To watch their poet dancing.
Arm in branch with willow tree,
Her laughter be everlasting.

The moon will smile, for never seen,
With dreams the poet dances.
Last waltz is saved, for the fairy queen,
This place be so enchanted.

Many words were born, on this very night,
Come to life by poet's dreaming.
Now they dance around the table light,
To rejoice their birth, their meaning.

Now all words can go where they please,
For they know the poet's feeling.
Some will laze upon warm summer breeze,
To await their poet's dreaming.

A P Feaver

A MEDITATION

When life has dismissed you
The caverns of time threaten
The helix of nature
Unleashes its venom
What then of reality known?
What new sense to be born
From that neuropathic maze
That hovers between hope and rejection?

Reflection of self
From long ago source
Drawn from the light
Of that infinite force
Born into poverty, strife and negation
Hope of a nation
Promised in faith to give new inspiration.

M Yockney

UNTITLED

He sits, a monument to age,
A young man in an old man's skin,
Time no longer waits for him.
A trembling lip, a bleary eye,
A parchment skin lined deep and long,
His step no longer sure and strong.
Hair long turned white and rather sparse,
Though neatly brushed with pride and care,
Before the mirrors alien stare.
His clothes though old and neatly brushes,
Hang loosely on his shrunken frame,
His joints are often wracked with pain.
Yet in his head he knows not age,
His arm is strong, his limbs are fleet,
His blood sings with his dancing feet.
He laughs at life, he joys with love,
His memory, like a treasure trove,
Replays his triumphs, hopes and loves
And in the secret places of his heart,
Where none can enter in and steal his joy,
He's once again a wild and hopeful boy.
He sits, a monument to age,
A young man in an old man's skin,
Time has no need to wait for him.

Caroline Isherwood

THE FINAL SECONDS

Forget the morn when I was born,
Forget the rides and moonlight tides
Forget the past, now fading fast,
Forget the dawn, the waving corn,
Forget I cried when a comrade died,
Forget the lies my heart derides.

Forget the skills, as a sail full fills,
Forget the screams of boyhood dreams,
Forget the strains, the pitiful gains,
Forget the thrills of night-time kills,
Forget the years of crocodile tears,
Forget the gleams of daylight beams.

Forget the lust, now dead as dust,
Forget the tears, the terror, the fears,
Forget the sighs, the lows, the highs,
Forget my trust in judgement just,
Forget the rain, my racking pain,
Forget goodbyes, and family ties.

Forget despair and the guilt I share,
Forget my will, unshaken still,
Forget my death and fading breath,
Forget my stare as I climb the stair,
Forget the gloom in this little room,
Forget until it's time to kill.

Forget the door I'll see no more,
Forget the slope, the smell of soap,
Forget the bell and Satan's hell,
Forget the hood, this trap of wood,
Forget all hope on this knotted rope,
        Forget.

Iolo Lewis

HONEY IN YOUR COFFEE

Sun, slowly retiring behind hills
Blushing with the heather
And freckled with the gold of gorse,
Heavy-lidded eyes espy
The sapphire and diamond sea
Caressing fine pale sand -
A gentle ocean making love with bejewelled kisses
There upon the empty beach.

Scents wafted from the driftwood fire
By a breeze so kind and warm
It insulates the dimming of the day:
Gentle whispers in the grass
Soft sighing of the sea,
Sea birds somewhere that talk amongst themselves
Of tides and fish and fish and tides and foam -
The hearing roams
And hears a subtle symphony
Played affectionately by the world.

A spreading smile, slow and smug
Bears witness to the grandeur of the present,
And in recollection of the taste
Of slowly smoked and flame-grilled fish
Fresh bread and butter,
And bliss - oh bliss, it comes to this:
Soft honey spooned with care
Into black coffee and sipped,
Sipped with relish while you watch
The day's events unfold
As they are painted on the wide canvas of our time.

Paul B Whittaker

GALACTIC IMPERIUM

Ten million suns the Star Kings hold,
Titanic wars are legends old.
Near forgotten space fleets rust,
War Lords of space, long turned to dust.
No fear of outer alien raids,
Conflict's barbaric splendour fades.
The Council rules with judgement wise,
Telepaths see through other's eyes.
The Age of Spaceships fades from thought,
Faster than light they teleport.
Machines and robots, long since gone,
Extinct, the monster cyclotron.
Man, self-sufficient, needs no tool,
Telekinesis is the rule.
The might of mind, the galaxy sways,
Serene, contented golden days,
The worlds of 'if' now real at last,
Pastoral worlds as in the past.

Evolution's cycles leap,
Expand into a wider sweep
As time unravels knot by knot
And man progresses on,
To what?

Clifford Pyves

TEACHER/PUPIL

I've composed a hundred lyrics about him in my head.
Written a thousand screenplays with every word he's said.
Stealing scenarios with him means a lot.
But it wouldn't be proper,
And it would never work,
Because he's young and I'm not.

I've sung a thousand love songs about us being apart.
I've acted a million scenes where he comes and claims my heart.
Crawling inside my dreams is the closest I'll ever be
Because it wouldn't be proper,
And it would never work,
Because he's young and I'm me.

Annie Marler

PARKINSON'S

I don't want to move from my armchair today,
Don't ask me what's wrong, I don't know.
They tell me that Parkinson's gets you this way.
The word that describes it is *no!*
No I don't! No, I can't! No I won't! No I shan't!
Is all that I find I can say.
This affliction creeps through like a strangling plant.
Is it going to plague me all day?

The stranger who sees me would think I'm a sham
And all the work's done by my wife.
I agree that it looks as if that's what I am
But the inference cuts like a knife.
An hour or two later I'm free of the gloom,
When it comes it is hard to endure.
The research into Dopamine will, we presume,
Give us hope for a permanent cure.

Later on when I'm tired and my legs start to quake,
I admit that I wish to be heard
But I can't find the words and my head starts to shake
And my efforts to talk sound absurd.
I suppose we are selfish and ask quite a lot
From our carers especially the wives.
We take them for granted - they're there on the spot
But who cares for *their* fractured lives?

Don Beale

MY BROTHER'S BANSHEE

The hour of darkness makes its call
My heart is prey to a stumbling fall
The banshee's call comes high and low
My tears, unheeded, start to flow
For love has lost this crucial fight
And cast on me, this darkest night
Yet guilty, as I face this stand
I fear so greatly, judgement's hand
Death will wear that blackened glove
As I fell so blindly to that of love
Such trickery and soft deceit
Temptation moved my helpless feet
I stood before the serpent's door
I should have loved my brother more
Yet there within, stood beauty's form
My passion spent in a raging storm
My brother's wife I had to own
Brotherly love has long since flown
Yet now in fear, his wife I hate
Her widow's finery reflect my fate
A death occurred in a brother's fight
I cringe as the rope is pulled too tight
I thought I saw a tear on her face
Yet that is covered by midnight lace

A figure dangles from a desolate tree
And now the banshee's curse is free.

J Aldred

WHILE YOU'RE AWAY

The tall, sad trees that saw you pass
So often, day by day,
Look wistfully as I go by
And sigh while you're away.

The silly swans beneath the bridge
That swim there every day,
Arch their long necks and droop their heads,
So sad while you're away.

Each wall and fence, each gate and door,
The pavement, cold and grey;
All things that knew your touch or sight,
Are sad while you're away.

The violin has lost its voice,
So vibrant, strong and gay;
It seems its very soul must sleep
And grieve while you're away.

I think the chair you used to have
Must now, so empty stay,
And holding out its empty arms,
Look sad while you're away.

Your books all stand upon their shelf,
So spectral, quiet and grey;
All these are but sad ghosts and shades
Of things while you're away.

Daphne Foreman

LOVE AWAKENED

A deep, dark shadow fell across my path,
As I stood alone in silent repose
Recalling events of years gone by
And of the day you handed me that beautiful red
Shining rose -
As red as the colour upon your cheeks -
A flower that gives pleasure,
As a fragrant flower speaks!
And thus love blossoms quickly
As the heart beats in time.
There was no question,
No rhythm or rhyme,
For the onrush of passion that engulfed my soul
As I studied your eyes gazing deeply into mine,
Transmitting their message of love,
Which, coupled with a sense of adoration and faith
That you were there for me all future time!
Would that it had lasted,
And your love alone was still mine!

Freda Ringrose

THE TRANSPLANT

Your heart is a gift
from a young man now dead.
Will love come adrift?
My youth, it must be said,
has passed. You swear by love,
that we shall never part
but *are* you my love
with an alien heart?

Peggy Trott

A TIME TO DIE

They say a man has never lived until it's time to die,
throughout his life, this man has learnt
to live, to laugh, to scream and cry.
As his life progresses he remembers his past dates
and he takes his journey to hell or pearly gates.
All his rights and all his wrongs are marked down
in a book,
together with the people and the path he took.
Did he live his live fully, as far as he could go?
Can he remember the people he was fortunate to know?
Will they still love him when he has passed on?
Will he be famous for poetry or song?
All the people who wronged him, will they feel sad
or will they feel guilty for treating him so bad!
Can he still see them from a seat up above?
Can he still speak to all the people he loved?
Will he see his family who passed on first?
Will his existence be better or worse?
So many questions that we cannot answer.
Is there really a God and do we call him master?
What will his children do now that he has gone?
And will life be cruel to them or will they live long?
Will he still have to worry about the right thing to do
Or does all his strength pass down to me and you?
Remember what I have said now as you life passes you by
and remember we all have a time to die.

D White

MY DAUGHTER AGED 4¾!

(To Amy)

Her eyes are green
To appreciate must be seen
Streaks of blond hair
Make her almost fair . . .
She grows tall,
And cries if she has a fall,
Desiring independence,
Sometimes, to great annoyance!
Learning, is her enjoyment,
Achieving, is her contentment,
Writing, provides stimulating insight . . .
Questions she will ask,
Require answers devoid of mask.
She has no fear,
But can be moved to shed a tear,
If a child were to cry,
Or someone close, to die . . .

Liz Edmonds

VIDEO VALIUM

To see it done on screen
Before it's done on you
The deft, white-gloved hands
Professional, sure
Metallic clink of released knife
Suddenly, red on white
Think of Hancock's
'That's almost an armful'
A false giggle, more maybe
Much more.

To remember it all over again
As one is on the operating table
Before obliterating mask descends
And it's you being done
A victim of video valium.

Bryn Bartlett

A LITTLE THOUGHT

Why is it only once a year
people are full of good cheer.
Smiling, greeting one and all,
gifts given out, when you call.

When a displaced child somewhere,
of Christmas, they are unaware.
Not for them, a special treat,
most of these, do not eat.

If some food does arrive,
a small morsel keeps them alive.
Starvation for another three weeks more
they forget what their mouth is for.

Spindly legs and swollen bellies,
this is where Hell really is.
So please remember once in a while
food freely given, is worth a smile.

A hungry child could have tasted
some of extra food that was wasted.
Across boundaries they are escorted.
How many deaths, go unreported?

Robert Thompson

A Teenage Cell

I started off as a teenage thief
The crimes got worse and life was sweet
I had money to spend although it weren't mine
I'd only got it from all the crimes
I became a hard thug and used a gun
I shot a man dead and thought I'd won.

But it's cold and lonely in this cell
The nights are long and the days are hell
I can see the sky through the cell bars
The nice blue sky and the clouds blowing past
The birds flying by and they are free
I wish I could spread wings and be
Just like the birds - flying free.

But it's cold and lonely in this cell
The nights are long and the days are hell
When I think back at the things I've done
And thought to myself. Oh yes, I've won
Then I see the bars on the window cell
And my life will end in a place called hell.

I pray to God to take me in
Forgive me for my life of sin
I pray that I will be forgiven
To live my next life in a place called Heaven.

Joy Willoughby

Shattered Lives

The day that broke so many hearts, that made a nation cry.
The question on a million lips cry loudly 'Dear Lord, why?'
The voices that no longer sing, the feet that will not dance,
of teachers and the little ones that never had a chance.

A day like any other but it ended in despair.
So many lives were shattered by just one who didn't care.
How can we start to comprehend the emptiness and pain,
of everyone that loved and lost the victims of Dunblane.

Ruth Bowles

THE COUNSELLORS

We sit before the Counsellors our problems to impart,
not quite knowing what to say, or even where to start.
We hope somehow their wisdom will help us see the light
that by the time our visits end, we'll almost have it right.
We fell into the big Black Hole along life's Milky Way,
of such despair and sorrow, that seemingly won't end.
It's very difficult to think life will be good again.

Because they care for mankind, they help us make amends
and kindly give us their spare time from family and friends.
So marriage guidance clients, listen when they say
eventually the sun will shine, a little day by day.
For not so very long ago I sat in that armchair
and I can well remember the despondency felt there.
Now those bad times are over, for me the sun shines through,
so believe them when they tell you it can happen for you too.

And to all the Counsellors from us all, I'd like to say
we really hope you live your lives a less complicated way.
But if you ever need an ear, just sit in that old chair,
and take in what your Counsellors say.
They're there because they care . . .

Beth Gardiner

ENDANGERED SPECIES

He used to roam our village streets
his purpose - to keep them clean and neat,
devouring bottles, bags and cans,
the now forgotten road-sweeping man.

Occasionally a noisy roar
heralds the mechanical brush,
trundling up and down the gutter
round parked cars, leaving litter
in its splutter.

Long-handled tweezers duly pick
tab-ends up between the nicks.
No long brush to sweep so neat
but pincer-armed he plods the street.

Today I saw the endangered species.
Long-handled broom, mobile bin,
foraging for a lunch-time treat.

Alas - he did not get his fill
he never came down my street!

Marjorie Upson

PRETTY POEMS

My pretty little poems in this
pretty little book,
It's all been wasted on their
turnout or look.

Written from a thought and tried
to apply some meanings,
but reading back they churned
out no feelings.

Such simple little words
and they fit in just fine,
and they each hold their own
childish little rhyme.

My pretty little poems will
always have other people's consent,
but the words written here
are never what I really meant.

James Deary

THE TWO O'CLOCK SHUDDER

The two o'clock shudder
Returned in full force at dawn.

He began to sweat profusely
As the new day awakened him.

Again
He started to experience the sense of alienation
That perception of his own non-humanity.
As it crept across the floor,
Mounted his bed, crawled up into his bones.
And finally, shuddered into his soul.

'To be alive at this time,'
He thought to himself,
As he lay in his perspiration soaked pyjamas,
'Is not to be a fully autonomous member of the human race.
It is not to be free but to be chained alive.'

Then the last thought that he had was
'This is the end.'
Before he returned to the individuality of his daily routine.

D Franks

FORGET MILES AND TRAVEL BY LIGHT YEARS

UFO's are flown by aliens who can travel by light years.
Their ancestors lived on this earth, 65 million years ago.
They left this planet to go to save other planets,
Although the Bible talks of Adam and Eve.
This book was a man-made book for one to read and follow,
But aliens brought mankind onto this earth,
From other planets far away in the Universe.
I would think the native black aboriginals were brought to
Australia first.
Next were brown Negroes in Africa,
Then thirdly the Chinese and continued so on,
That's why each group of people speak differently.
Of course we were born on this earth
But it was our first ancestors who were brought here by the aliens,
The Evening Star today (16.4.99) page 6 speaks of racism.
Well as we all came from different planets, we must learn to respect
one another.
Yesterday's papers (15.4.99) said a breakthrough of a new solar
system was found.
Of three huge planets, 44 lights years from earth, on the Milky
Way belt.
Also yesterday in Sydney, Australia had hailstones, size of lemons.
Freak weather in 1987 had hailstones in the summer, around
Ipswich, Suffolk.
This weather is caused by aliens that have been in the area.
See aliens in UFO's travel by means of atomic power which
caused freak weather.
There are a billion stars in the Universe.
A star lives 10 millions years then explode and then form a planet.
There are millions of planets like ours, up there.
Mankind must forget travelling in miles,
And start to travel by light years in order to go and investigate them.
The word God is short for the word Universe.

There are at least a million Universes up there,
And everything is made by the Universe.
Rings round a planet are rocks, and if one goes off the ring, it then
goes through space as a comet.

E M Thompson

JUST ANOTHER DAY . . .

It's been a funny sort of day, one way and another,
it started when the postman brought a letter from my brother.
He said 'There isn't any stamp, which means you'll have to pay,
and it's double the amount please!' What a good start to my day!

My brother wants to come and stay, a week or two he said,
that means I'll have to sort things out, and get ready my spare bed.
Then round about lunchtime, a knock came on my door,
and when I went to answer it I found a note upon the floor.

It said 'Could I help next Saturday at a jumble sale in town.'
Well I've never been approached before, it really made me frown.
Then I decided to go shopping which made me feel quite jolly,
until I came to pushing round the supermarket trolley.

It seems I should have passed a test to get the trolley round the store,
I badly judged a left hand bend and cans scattered to the floor.
On escaping with my shopping and back safely in my car,
I thought I'd visit my friend Rose, as she doesn't live too far.

But when I reached her cottage, no car was parked outside.
With all the doors and windows closed, I knew it was a wasted drive.
Now as I sit at home again and drinking cups of tea,
I wonder how on earth these things always happen just to me.

E Rendell

ALAS . . .

Kenny was a climber
from the time he was a tot.
Before he learned to toddle
he was climbing in his cot.

When he progressed to toddling
he was climbing everywhere,
and his antics over furniture
drove his mother to despair.

At school he was the champion
at climbing trees and walls.
And always greatly in demand
for retrieving far-flung balls.

At college he was notable
for scaling every tower,
and leaving some momento there
as token of his power.

And then his finest moment came,
they offered him a place.
In a team to climb Mount Bongo
by a yet - unconquered face.

But pride doth go before a fall
as we have oft heard tell.
He tried to scale the Pearly Gates
but slipped
          and fell
            and fell.

Heather Brackley

ROSE-TINTED SPECTACLES (YEAR 1999)
(A Necessity In Life No-One Should Be Without)

My rose-tinted spectacles
have mislaid once again.
Strange how without them
things do not appear quite the same.

Rainbowed sparkling glass
gilt-edged golden frames.
Where did I leave them?
Were here yesterday.

Usually much laughter
come what may.
Look on the bright side of life.
Feel grumpy today.

Unsociable in-laws
seemed friendly before.
Neighbours are bitching.
Why? I'm not sure!

People unsmiling
when glancing my way.
Crestfallen, gloomy
nothing cheerful to say.

Searched each nook and cranny
let's try under the cat.
Found my rose-tinted spectacles.
Thank goodness for that!

Audrey P Stapley-Williams

DOCTRINE OF AN INTROVERTED PIN
(With a leer at Lear!)

Metal and sausage must go hand in hand,
Ferdinand's nightie is shredding a strand.
Need he pretend that he's buried in sand?
It's almost a muffler or two!

Speaking of bats, it's a uniform shame.
To boo them and stew them and set them aflame,
It's nearly as bad when a lettuce goes lame,
There's always a flag painted blue.

And that is the reason I rattle all night,
Juggling with venison (buttoned up tight).
And even on Mondays, I don't think it's right,
To embarrass a cow with the flu!

If only an answer would come to me quick!
Like gangsters unravelling a long piece of brick.
I'm sure I could thrash it without being sick,
And you know what a poodle can do!

G O'Neil

JUST A TREE!

I've been standing here
for fifteen years,
birds, they land on me,
and bellow right down my 'ears'.

During the spring,
bees, they swarm on every branch,
after my beautiful blossom,
I had 'ten' stings on my last count!

When autumn comes,
the birds come 'again',
pecking my branches,
I'm telling you, that's real pain.

So here I stand,
through the cold and wet.
Oh! Don't 'you' worry about 'me'!
After all, I'm only a 'tree'!

Karen Grady

A GUIDED WALK

Have you got your brolly dear?
As we're going for a walk
Don't stand in that puddle dear
While you listen to the talk.

Pay attention to the history dear
Above the traffic roar
Another half-day outing dear
This one door to door.

Whenever rain is falling dear
Or when the skies are grey
That's when we all meet up dear
To wend our weary way.

So it was on that Friday dear
When we strode out with the Mayor
To tread the streets of Salisbury dear
Pausing here and there.

Difficult to remember dear
All that was revealed
But much is there to see dear
If eyes are just kept peeled.

Kathleen H Allen

LA FILLE ET LA MORTE

Two things truly fascinate me,
       the girl and death;
with blond tresses long and eyes blue to see,
       she, my consciousness, is my breath,
she haunts every day and every night,
       I ache to see her, feel her close,
she's the spirit inspiring these words recite,
       she's so young, skin smooth and pilose;
I think of the phases that are her life,
       and wonder at all she's becoming,
I dream to see the man to whom she be wife,
       the man this flower'll be blooming,
I read of adolescent changes afoot,
       the ways developing body time flows,
so much happening to beauty, this tenderfoot,
       adult in few years, the universal tableaux;
And my thoughts drift to the socially heretic,
       her physical self and attraction,
that eye the perfection of love allotropic,
       and repeat in my mind that action;
I took a trip to the end of my mind,
       I found a place secret and cool,
I started out after senses found unkind,
       and that girl became another's jewel,
the realm by Barrie named 'Neverland'
       lonely, drugged by the past,
the place where for four years did I stand,
       waiting, hoping the loneliness not last;
here I am waiting for the last breath,
       seeking, thoughtlessness and death.

L E Dinemuro

SINE QUA NON

The stars they shine and light my way
My life if loud, I cannot escape.
I've run so far to find I've begun
The journey back to this thing I abhor.
The screams from Heaven tell me to wrong,
My head and my rhythm, they have grown sore.
Bandage my aches, I can't help myself,
And wound my pain, deliver me to light.
I have arrived, it's time to begin.
Wait for me under the ground,
The quakes will summon us once more.
Rise up to the sun and fight the warring moons,
And remind them of all the hurt they cause themselves.
Then leave them all behind to live or to die as they please.
To begin or to end; yet which is which
This ends, every time.

Danielle Green

WISH YOU WERE HERE

We have been apart
for nearly a year
you have found someone else
to whisper in your ear
To hold you so tight
when the winter is near
To laugh and joke
when the summer is here

I wonder if you ever think of me
and our year
I really do miss you
and wish you were here

Rachel Wake

THE LITTLE GIRL

The little girl sat on the bank, catching butterflies
but looking closer at the child, tears were in her eyes.
Although above the sky was blue and the sun was beating down
tomorrow she's be moving on, leaving her home and town.
Leaving the garden she loved so much, the stream running just outside
and as she sat and thought of this, again the small child cried.

A trader walking down the lane, with horse and cart in tow
stopped and chatted to the child and asked what ailed her so?
She told of the sadness of leaving the house,
and all of her friends in the street.
She told of the fear that she felt deep inside,
of the strange new place and people she'd meet.
She told of how she'd been born in this town,
and how all of this she would miss -
the trader sat and pondered awhile and then his reply was this;
'Although far away you might travel, your heart it will stay in
your home and when you are an adult and able, can return to
where you had grown.'
This made the young girl feel much better,
the thought of maybe returning one day
and the trader just tipped his hat to the child,
and said he must be on his way.

The women went off in a daze now, drifting back into the tale
at 90+ and the life she'd had, she'd become very weak and quite frail.
But still a glint was in her eyes to tell of the day she went home
and the happiness she felt then - to return to where she had grown.
She remembered the kindly old trader, his words meant
a lot now and then and this women of 90 something - had gone
back to the girl of just 10 . . .

L Bristow

OUR BABIES

Our babies are our treasures
A wonder to behold
Both soft and cute and caring
Courageous, strong and bold.

They shake when we got out to work
They bark when we come home
They ask to go out quite a lot
But never far to roam.

Our babies are getting older now
A thought that brings us sorrow
We try not to dwell on that though
Just look forward to tomorrow.

Such joy two dogs have never brought
We love them through and through
And in our hearts we'll always have
Our Danny and our Blue.

V J Aldridge

HAIKU FORCES

The wind in gusts
Blowing like a train
But into every nook and cranny

The rain it falls
Into hedgerows like leaves
Then flows to reservoir

The sun it glares
Like a devil
Though it is a comfort

Orry Drinkwater

A NOVEMBER DAY

The dawn breaks on a very still cold morning,
everywhere is covered with a sharp frost.
The skies are a mixture of red, blue grey and white,
with a slight mist hanging around the tops of the trees.
This is a cold November day.

As the morning passes
everyone hustles about, all wrapped up warmly.
It is so cold that their breath appears like steam.
Small children are running to keep warm.
The winter days are approaching fast.

At night people are snug in their warm homes.
Smoke appears from chimneys
and the windows are all steamed up.
Soon everyone will be tucked up in bed.
The lights will go out and everywhere will be quiet.

Only the sound of animals moving about will be heard
and everyone sleeps.
It is a silent world for a few hours.
After which another November day will dawn.

Margaret Wood

SUMMER

Summer, and the droning of a fat bee is
Magnified as, laden with pollen,
It shimmies inside
A foxglove's face.

Even the neighbouring cats ignore
The sparrow's chirping
On the lawn,
Though peeping through watchful eyes.

Wind-chimes play a melody
As an occasional breeze rifles over
The garden, saturating the air with the scents of
Stocks, roses, pinks and lavender.

As evening approaches, large flocks of birds
Head toward a nearby coppice,
Swooping and diving in a cerulean-tinged sky.
Shadows lengthen; languorously, the sun sinks out of sight
On a lone, cushioning cloud.

Betty Morton

THANKSGIVING

The bells are ringing
in the old village church
on this special harvest morn;
The choir boys are hurrying
through the lychgate,
woe betide any boy late.
They must be on cue
when the organ strikes up.
The church is bedecked
with flowers bright and gay.
All chosen from the gardens
of the village folk, this day.
For this harvest home array.
Produce brought off the land
where everyone lent a hand.
Fruit, vegetables
colours of autumn
like a golden band
brought to church
a bounty, off the land.

M Parnell

CHILDHOOD POND

When silver streaks the willow trees
The pools are cool and deep;
A dragonfly bedecks the sky;
The morning is asleep.

The leaves shine in the speckled sun;
The dragonfly floats by.
Whisky as dandelion-down
A vapour soon to die.

The skater on the pond will not be there
Tomorrow, or much after,
Tracing its patterns on the skin
Of childhood and our laughter.

The mushroom hides and dries inside the grass;
The distance cow-pat imitates its form -
Reflects the sun, its flat, white mass
Attracting thunderflies on to its warm
Caked skin, while down, down, down, within the colder green,
A roach meanders, pushing back a frond,
A willow-root, to draw the curtains
On my childhood pond.

J Adams

MY KEEPER

Oh, what it's like to find yourself in a situation
where you have only imagined it.
The purest thought, a simple touch.
A world which stops, a time which doesn't exist.

Those eyes which shine so bright but look so deep
and touch my soul.
Those lips which make me smile and kiss so sweet
to warm my pounding heart.

He has looked for me and I for him.
But never the twain had met.
Until luck, fate, God whichever you believe in
threw two broken hearts together.

For you are my dream come true.
You are my love so deep.
You . . . the keeper of my heart,
mind, body and soul.

Maria Conte

CASSIE

Feline fantasies,
Smooth milky cream
Soft cloudy bed,
Rich silky dream
Large liquid eyes,
Deep velvet pools
Heavenly promises,
Cunningly fools
Perpetual paws
Poetically stanced
Beautiful body
Skilfully danced
Curious behaviour
Sensuous, sublime
Deviously cautious
Perfectly timed
Wickedly wise,
Wantonly free
Majestic and proud
Captivates me!

L Jones

(FOR FRED) - DIAMOND MEMORIES

I can't believe is it really true?
Sixty years since I said *'I do.'*

We had no photographs, no cake,
My wedding dress I had to make.

I close my eyes so I can see,
My memories flood back to me.

We faced a war and hardship too,
Heartbreak came when God took you.

I can't believe is it really true?
Thirty years since I lost you.

My only love, we're not apart,
You're locked forever in my heart.

Age shall not wither, or the years condemn.
Forever young, till we meet again.

Mary Hutson

APRIL

What other month can be so fickle
As April who deceives
The bright sun draws sap
That rises in the leaves.

When blossom bursts to life
April hides a blow
Springing forward plants
Suddenly cut by snow.

Those cutting wintry showers
Nights with April frost
Such eagerness to grow
The blossom's cause is lost.

Cut as with a sickle
Sharp as any knife
Such promise from the flowers
Too soon and what a cost.

Jenny Major

HANAMI AND HAIKU TIME

When springtime comes and Hanami
Sakura beauty eyes shall see,
A fragrant land in magic sway,
Sakura-saku, here today!

Let senses drink the blossom's dew
To fill the heart with love anew,
And turn away from winter's gloom
To breathe the sweetness of the bloom.

Kimonos ladies touched by bliss
Greet sweet Sakura with a kiss.
For they can see the time is now
When freshness bends the graceful bough.

Beneath the trees enjoying rest
Hearts welcome spring, their loving guest.
For time has cast aside the bud
Releasing dreams in joyous flood.

In Hanami when hearts beat fast
Sakura love with splendour cast.
Throughout Japan with blooms sublime,
Then Hanami is Haiku time!

Peter James O'Rourke

WHY!

Why is this world such a troubled place
All this hatred and talk of race.
We all have one life for as long as it lasts
We should go on remembering things of the past.

Not all things were right that caused us to fight
But if only people would talk and listen
and take heed of what happened in those dark nights.

Why can't people be happy with their own little lot
instead of scheming and intent to plot, to hurt and
destroy all the good in this world before into
infinity we all are hurled.

M Pullan

THE DANCE OF THE LONELY DAFFODIL

In the distance beyond the wilderness
I can see their radiant golden glow
Warming all that surrounds them.
I appear the same, but I dance alone.

I raise my head and contemplate their feelings.
Their contentment reels through the breeze,
Engaging a butterfly in a waltz, before slowly
Drifting towards me.

Their happiness shadows my loneliness
And taunts my vulnerable blossom.
My purity is exposed, defenceless,
As your unity dominates the glory of the dance.

Claire C Dick

THE LAST LETTER

Sylvia's final written words reveal her personality,
Her great courage in the face of adversity,
The love of plant propagation,
Her joy at the result of cultivation,
The urn of blue scillars planted in the fall,
The exotic amaryllis grown so tall,
The friendly squirrel who came to her door,
Birds she fed, who will see her no more,
Hatred of loud music causing lack of concentration,
But complaints never brought satisfaction,
Affection for family and friends all her days,
Intense interest in their welfare always,
Sylvia's pen is now laid to rest,
Thankful I am to have her last letter - the best.

I L Wright

AUTUMN

Grey clouds chased across a stormy sky,
by a wind vicious and powerful reaching high.
Leaves fly and swirl, drifting everywhere,
torn from hedge and tree, tossed into the air.
The sky ever-changing, dramatically bold,
the wind now triumphant, with its strong hold
over all that lies before it, powerless to fight,
buffeting and bullying everything in sight.
Challenging the wind, the sun shines through.
Changing grey to gold with an unusual hue.
The lightening sky now shows a friendly face,
appealing to the eye, overtaking the wind's pace.
Sunshine sparkles on the lake, the wind reduced to a breeze.
The forest floor a carpet of red and gold leaves.

Valerie Ansell

THE CRUEL SEA

'Anchors Aweigh lads. Anchors Aweigh,'
The voice of the captain was heard to say.
Family and friends stood on the quay,
And waved as the ship sailed out to sea.

The breeze was warm as they made headway,
On calm waters that summer's day.
Then on the sixth day, the wind blew a gale,
It rocked the vessel . . . passengers became seasick and frail.

The swell of the ocean was strong,
As it tossed and pushed the ship along.
The deck was awash with waves mountainous high,
'We're headed for the rocks!' came someone's cry.

The screams were deafened by the breaker's roar,
Everyone prayed they were near the shore.
Some jumped overboard as mayhem broke out upon the deck,
Others managed to scramble into boats before the ship was wrecked.

They looked on in horror as the ship was dashed,
Against jagged rocks the vessel smashed.
With a gigantic hole in its side
The ship gurgled, then sank beneath the tide.

The survivors rowed for dear life,
But the cruel sea claimed another - someone's wife.
They huddled together hoping to be found,
But the sea showed no mercy as it tossed the boat around.

The victims became weaker - survival wasn't good,
For they had gone too long without water and food.
The grey mask of death was on many a face,
A watery grave was *their* final resting place.

The cruel sea waited, to swallow the remaining few,
When - a mast came into view.

Maj Macaulay

LINCOLNSHIRE COUNTRY CLOVER

Clear, white mountain light
Showered the fields
On a perfect day, in a nectar laden, magical may.

Wrapped in a blanket of buttercups,
The earth heaved up its plump cherry blossom.
Pink, smothering the tree.
As far as I could see
Was rape seed yelling yellow in flat chequered fields
And virgin air filled the senses,
Blown in from an azure sea.

Red, chiffon poppies danced
Amid a purple evening hue
Dissolving away into morning dew on another May day,
Blissful bountiful and new.

Claire Fitzgerald

WINTER SUNSET

Who painted
The sky
Tonight?
Turquoises
Through to
Navy.
Carmine red
Through to
Coral.
Indigo
Clouds float
Along.

Angela Pritchard

Our Garden

We have no grass in our garden
For we're not able to give it care
We have slabs, stones and other things
So it doesn't always look so bare.

There are two squirrels in our garden
By the names of Denzil and Sam,
But I must say they are cast in stone
And I love them because I am.

An animal lover of course
Of both the living and the other sort
But not having facilities for the living
Our stone ones have to be bought.

Korky the koala sits under the tree
A eucalyptus tree it must be said,
Next to Felix the black stone cat,
Watching over our small spread.

There is a wishing-well there too
By a heather covered rockery mound
And this is more or less the full extent
Of our small piece of garden ground.

Gerard Oxley

Misty Blue

When I gaze into your loving eyes,
I'm entranced by misty blue;
When *you* look into *my* eyes, sweetheart,
What looks back at you?

D'you see all the loving, the yearning, the caring?
D'you see all my wanton desires?
Or does passion show, with that deep inner glow,
Fuelled and flamed by affectionate fires?

Steve Sutton

MUSIC

Song and verse and musical sounds
Are just a few of the good sounds around.
Opera is a classic musical play
Some people don't like it, it's boring they say.

Song and verse and musical sounds
Are just a few of the good sounds around.
Rock'n'Roll is what you jitterbug-bug to,
Some people dress in suits and shoes - usually blue.

Song and verse and musical sounds
Are just a few of the good sounds around.
Mowtown and Soul bring out the love in us all,
When in love, these are the ones that we recall.

Song and verse and musical sounds
Are just a few of the good sounds around.
Heavy rock is for greasers and bikers alike,
These have long hair, and head-bang all night.

Song and verse and musical sounds
Are just a few of the good sounds around.
All are different, rock, soul, opera and pop,
Just get right down to it, and bop till you drop.

Sue Kami

LOST LOVE

How could I forget those soft lips that once touched mine,
The love, the friendship that stood the pace of time.
The warmth of your body, so gentle, so divine,
Since that day we first met I knew you would be mine.
Our love together we would share and give,
To be together again, just once more I wish.
To hold you tightly once more in my loving arms,
And melt into your beauty, love and charms.
Together you made my life so complete and sweet,
But deep down within my heart I knew your love I couldn't keep.
Then came that day so full of sadness and sorrow
For the pain I felt in my heart, how could there be a tomorrow.
That tearful day when you said goodbye,
All we both could do was kiss each other and cry.
Now that time has passed me by and the years have gone,
The memories of you in my heart will always live on.

Allan Young

THE GREAT ENGLISH BREAKFAST

A sensible way to start the day
Is a jolly good breakfast for all.
It sets you up for the rest of the day
And keeps you on the ball.

Nice crisp bacon, an egg or two,
A sausage and mushrooms as well.
Then a nice cup of tea to follow
Will always go down well.

Never mind the rolls and jam,
Continental, with edges all curled.
With a great English breakfast inside you
You're ready to face the world.

P Anderson

HOME TO A VIRUS

I have been given notice to quit,
told to leave my home,
but it's so warm and healthy here,
and I have room to grow.

Healthy kidneys, healthy limbs,
I can run so free,
'Cos, I'm a little virus, and I grow,
just like a tree.

Most landlords, when they know I'm here,
give up and let me stay.
But this one says, 'Oh no you're not,
out you go today.'

When the pain gets bad, instead of shouting out,
she gets up and exercises,
and keeps on walking about.
This one is going to do battle with me,
of that there is no doubt.

It doesn't matter where I stray,
she counteracts me in some way.
So I've been told to quit, to leave, today,
got to move, find somewhere new . . .
You look healthy . . . Can I come to you?

Anne Willingale

A FRIENDLY SMILE

Love and laughter, smiles and tears,
Days go by, weeks and years.
Live each day, as it is meant,
With happiness and content.

All it takes is a friendly smile
To someone lonely, it makes life worthwhile.
For someone sad, a good day make
A kindly word is all it will take.

A helping hand to those in need
Just look around and heed.
The day's not wasted, but worthwhile
If upon a face you leave a smile.

And when day has ended, and you sit and dream
Do not think of what might have been.
Just look around, and your blessing see,
At the love, and contentment that surrounds thee.

V M Foulger

SOFTEE

I cut the daisies down today
I threw them in the sack,
And from within the mangled weeds
One bloom reproached my back.

I could feel its pained expression
Follow me down the path,
I tried to casually ignore it -
All the family did, was laugh.

I thrust my fingers deep, deep down,
To rescue the petalled life
That silently called aloud to me,
And caused such mental strife.

I popped it in a vase so tall,
And placed it on the sill.
I never thought a single bloom
Could give me such a thrill.

Gwen Place

TALKING TIME

Are you without a voice?
Will you ever find the courage to speak?
You are the human form of white noise
who thrives on the fear of the weak.

You became the invisible face at the window
and every sudden breeze was your icy breath,
In the darkest night you moved in shadows
and in dreams, you were the instrument of death.

In the crowded street you were a stranger's glance
or the stalker watching and waiting in every parked car,
You stumbled upon your victim purely by chance,
but this time you went too far.

Now you're paying the price with precious time
after you were declared the loser of the silence game,
Caught in the act by a trace on the line,
they clocked your number and the judge got your name.

Kathleen Speed

AFTERNOON INTERLUDE

The hiss of a grass snake
green no danger,
no need to take precautions.
She lay back listening
to the murmuring of
the breeze in the heather,
as they made music together.
Felt the warm sun's caresses,
heard the noise of the cicadas,
their legs brushing together.
Only later when the danger
became incarnate
and the fruit from the
virgin seed burst forth,
did the sound of the cicadas
fuse into the cry of a child
and her smile for a while
held the memory
of warm sun
and an afternoon
long over and done.

Polly Bennison

LULLABY FOR MORK AND MINDY

Sleep, little cats, with paws tight curled
Sleep, little cats, in your own little world.

Dream of the mice you caught today
Dream of the birds that got away.

Dream of the dogs you put to flight
When you make it clear you were out for a fight.

Dream of the fish you'd like to eat
And the sweet green grass beneath your feet.

Sleep, little cats, so safe and snug
Whether on armchair, bed or rug.

When morning breaks, come sun or rain,
Tiny tigers will wake to play again.

E Lamberton

POETRY COMPETITION

to stand a chance my friend said don't
write it out in rhyme
prose is much preferred so
write your essay out and then chop
it into uneven lines and please
don't worry about how each line
ends

But they like it to 'look' like a poem

don't put in emotion, that's passé
nature's a turn off too
avoid being topical that's a
mistake lots of the losers make

but most of all don't be up
front
if it's easy to understand
you've had it
be obtuse be oblique be strange think
Picasso think calves in formahaldehide
don't give it an end
just leave it

K Jenkins

SILENCE OF THE GUNS

Now only the wind sings
to the beat of vultures' wings,
stars still shine on,
but the Cowboys are all gone.

Once across the plains they rode,
tough men in days of old,
by their guns they lived or died
as death danced by their side.

To snowy hills of Montana
or stabbing heat of Arizona
where stark the cacti stand
as sentinels in desert sand.

Mumbled prayers were said
for the Cowboys dead,
for the fights they had lost
their lives were the cost.

Time has taken its toll,
now only ghost balls roll.
Hooves no longer pound,
guns no longer sound.

The wide men of the West
are now gone to their rest.
They staked their claim
to always remain
in American history,
part truth, part mystery.

Anna Punshon

'WAR: READ ALL ABOUT IT'

A pale blue woolly hat frames a frowning face
Of a young boy with large brown eyes.
An ordinary, familiar face.
In the background, a child in a bouncy coat
Looks back at the camera from its mother's arm
From within the crowd.
The people wear ordinary 'British' clothes; it is cold.
I notice a plastic coated pushchair.
The boy smells smoke, gunpowder
and the dirty unwashed smell of the musty people
irritated by each other as arms and elbows dig into them.
The boy wonders where he will sleep tonight
And licks his furry unbrushed teeth.
Amidst the sound of firing,
Only the echo of his memories can be heard:
The relentlessly fading vision of home.
They have left behind a teenage diary,
A favourite book, wedding photos, a banker's card,
A husband, wife or child.

'A stark choice: abandon their homes or face extermination'.

Cathy Wade

THE COUNTDOWN 'GLAMOUR PUSS'

Carol you are a dainty doll
With your skirt above your knee
Your shapely legs so stunning
Wish they belonged to me!!!!
What a treat for us at home
And in the studio too
Who is this Richard Whiteley?
When we can gaze at you.

Esther Hawkins

TREASURES OF AUTUMN

Trees standing tall on the skyline as nature comes gathering her dues,
Leaves from each one gently falling, a pattern of soft blended hues.
So many birds have migrated, but many still will remain.
Magpie, the sparrow, the robin, search enough food to obtain.
Squirrels are gathering nut crop, hoarding against winter's cold,
Mole lining nest with some soft grass nods a good day to field vole.
Badger is hurrying homeward wanting to be where it's warm,
Don't venture out very often preferring to stay where it's calm.
Moorhens out on the river swim with the duck and the swan,
Carefully eyeing the water till unwary fish comes along.
Blackberries grow in the hedges, picked they enhance apple pies,
Chestnuts can be very tasty, roasted beneath open skies.
So much to see and remember, carry us through till the spring.
So many wonders to gaze at no price to pay for each thing.
Red, green and browns all surround us, plus silver of river's gleam,
Each season has special glory, this is the finest it seems.
Grandest of all nature's treasures spread in a mantle of love,
Sharing each one with another, gifts from our God up above.

Barbara Goode

I MISS HIM

Nearly two hundred miles away as the crow flies
A part of me remains.
The pain which has enveloped me
Now only throbs - no one can see
How much I miss him.

I speak his name quite normally
Accept good wishes and congratulations.
He's doing fine, he's fit, he's well
I just wish it didn't hurt like hell
That he's away
And how I miss him.

I have two others in my nest
To tend and clothe and feed.
For them things remain the same,
They're loved and have all they need.
But my home won't be the same again
Until he returns to the fold . . .
Till then I miss him.

Beverley Griffin

FENLAND GEM

East Anglia is an area of great renown,
Within its bounds there's many delightful towns,
Set in the flat fen, *Peterborough* is a gem.
The skies are crowned with Cathedral spires,
Such a glory enlightens all our desires,
Perhaps the monks of old still pray,
Within the Cathedral walls their spirits stay,
This holy place Henry the Eighth saved,
So today we can visit a queen's grave.
Old and new buildings blend,
In the city we can shop and greet friends,
A stroll along the Nene river banks,
Gives us a reason to give thanks,
All around we see past history,
This lovely city is no mystery,
Ride upon the Nene Valley steam train,
It will bring back memories again,
There's so many sights to see
Lots of fun for all the family
For a holiday or for a day
Peterborough is a really grand place to stay.
Don't delay make your way, come today.

Kathleen Fry

NURSES

I give thanks to all the nurses who looked after me,
They were all absolute angels you see,
There's never a minute to spare,
When you have lots of patients who need your care,
They always approach with a smile,
Though they're tired and worn out, they're in denial,
There just so dedicated to the work they do,
Still caring and smiling when they're feeling blue,
Doing a job a cut above the rest,
They surely do deserve the best,
If only everyone realised they deserve more pay,
Not next month, next year, but now today,
Why did they choose the job they do,
Helping others, they are the chosen few,
So if nurses you wish you'd chosen another career,
Don't because in our hearts you're very dear,
It's thanks to you we thrive and live,
So all our heartfelt wishes to you we give.

Trudy Lapinskis

DUMBFOUNDED!

Excitedly she undid the parcel
One wrapper after another
A mountain of paper lay
On the floor
So soon she was to discover
A tiny fragment lay in the box
She faintly sat on the stool
The words on the parchment
Suggestively said
Oh what an April Fool!

Theresa Eady

MORE

More than the faintest hint of your scent
the echo of the last kiss
and the ghost of your embrace.
A twice weekly meeting,
a few snatched minutes on the phone.
Otherwise alone, separated by distance
by work and more pressing commitments.
Goodbyes are becoming harder
but some things remain unchanged.
I take you as you are
What is on offer
for fear of failure in losing what we have.
Aspirations left unsaid.
Hoping that time will change the pace
of this love affair.

Nicola Grant

THE STREAM
(Written in tears)

The sun is shining brightly
High up in the sky.
I look down at the water
As the reflections go floating by.
I ask myself - what is wrong with me?
I never get an answer - it goes floating down to the sea.
I look up high into the sky, and I ask the Lord above?
Am I taking the right road - the road that leads to love?
I never get an answer - I don't know the reason why.
Perhaps it's just because . . .
                    They keep on floating by.

Chris Longwith

ANGELS WITHOUT WINGS

I have friends in high places
I guess you might say
they wear no uniform
Nor do they have airs and graces
They wear no crown
No riches or palaces
        Yet friends in high places
        I know I have
they look like you and I
        no don't sigh
they wear jeans and T-shirts
        and maybe carry a mobile phone
        they're on call
        they visit you at home
listening with patience
        understanding your pain
with nothing for them to gain
        they pick up the pieces
        when your life is left in ruin
they hold out the hand of friendship
        they give you your room
        making you see sense
        of crazy nonsense
encouraging you to talk
when all you want to do is walk
        they're God's guardian angels
        placed on this Earth
the gift of understanding
        they have from birth
        no visible halo
        no wings not yet
        yet friends I have in high places
            you bet

Yvette Herbert

RUNNING IN THE RAIN

We hoped it would be sunny on our Fun Run day,
But Bank Holidays are always wet,
In the merry month of May,
So I wore my mac and wellies,
When I finally went.
To cheer on the friend I'd sponsored.
Then I lunched in the tent,
I tried to take a photo,
Of the Pearly King and Queen,
As throwing custard pies at folk,
Is really not my scene.
Radio Cambridgeshire was broadcasting on the air.
But standing in the endless rain,
Was more than I could bear.
So home I pedalled with my purchases and plants,
To have a hot bath and maybe snatch a chance,
To catch up on my letters and watch TV.
Then my friend tapped on the door,
And 'Can I' said he,
'Have one pound twenty pence for my laps.'
So I gave him his money saying,
'Well done chaps,
And lasses, all for raising without fuss,
Money for some comforts,
For folk worse off than us.'

D Bacon

TO BE AN AUCTIONEER

If another chance at life I had,
(I hear them cry 'Oh spare us Dad')
But if I did get another go, this secret I've kept hid,
My application I'd write differently, put in another bid.
An auctioneer that's what I'd be,
Never the like will you ever see.
A slap on the leg, a 'Have you all done',
Lots one to nine hundred, I'd sell every one.
The hammer held high, my eyes rolling round
To catch every movement and hear every sound.
Each wink, each nod, each finger raised,
I wouldn't fail to see,
And as the bids grew higher, I'd be thinking of my fee!
At the end of the day, all worked up and hot,
I'd boast of the way I'd got rid of the lot.
Rubbish and treasures, all fought for and sold,
To farmers and gents, men both young and old.
It's the dream that I have as my garden I dig,
Still, later this evening, I could sell my pig!!

Dorothy Hadley

BESIDE THE RIVER'S EDGE

As I sit here beside the quiet water's edge,
I look to my future with worry and dread.
Down here it is so quiet, tranquil and peaceful,
Except for the odd squawk of a swan or tiny seagull.

I listen to its rhythm, the music that it plays,
I love its calming, soft and mild ways.
Sitting here alone I have time for reflection, time to think and time to
dream,
My life seems so empty, just one flowing stream.

As night-time falls upon the river and I see it's shining rays,
I think about my long and painful days,
I reminisce and begin to shed some painful tears,
My life is unspeakably empty and heading nowhere.

But soon my mind begins to clear,
I no longer ponder my future with dread and fear.
While the sun sets in the blue satin sky, the wind begins to groan,
And as the world still goes on turning I no longer feel alone.

Emma Pickering

OUR LOVE IN GOD

Being a true Christian,
    Means doing the right thing always,
We still love our neighbour,
    As ourselves, throughout the days,
Christianity, means to be loving,
    And caring, also forgiving,
We must keep our true thoughts,
    In our hearts within,
And never to make fun,
    Of our prayers,
    When we pray to God,
We must make sure, that we love him dearly,
    And to make things good,
We can do our best, for our Saviour,
    By saying, 'The Lord's Prayer,'
He will then forgive us,
    Our mistakes, and sins,
And help us to live,
    And pass in peace,
    Through blowing winds . . .

J A Shaw

THE HERON

Brazen, metallic sun arrows down
Into the fractured, jagged water.
Diffused light, glittering and splintered
Dances and trembles on the shimmering surface.
The heron, mute, enigmatic sentinel of his riverside domain
Stoically and silently meticulously scans the hazardous lake and shore.
A sudden reverberation and the mystic watcher rises
And orbits the lake in reverent trajectory
Slate wings hood and beat a tattoo over the restless surface.
Cutting the water with incising glance into the satin depths of piscine
                                                              promise.
Deliberately skimming on velvet, tender feathers of steel
He pursues his chosen path!
The farthest shore is gained and captured
And in this vaporous kingdom of sedge and rush
With unblinking and obdurate stare he reigns supreme!

Ann Eaves

SUMMER STORM

Walking, stifled by silence
under the iron sky hung
with clouds like grey rags,
across soaked grass cringeing
and pulling underfoot,
to face twin enemies:
jealousy in a lightning flash
brighter than a cat's eyes,
fear in the thunder beating
in my chest. The line of hills
stands, much too close, on guard.
Don't tell me to cross a field is hard.

Michael Collins

FOREVER

The heat haze
Shimmered across the lake
The hills appearing as
a mirage, in the distance

The sun was a huge
orange ball, hung in the sky
And far away
the muted sounds of voices

I watched the condensation
form on your glass
Touching it gently
I ran my finger down

It was cool
like a raindrop
As it ran over my finger
and dripped on the table

You raised the glass
your tongue touching the liquid
Like a woman's mouth
as you tasted and enjoyed

And I felt the pulse
in my throat
Like the trembling heart
of a wild bird

You touched my hand
And I rolled all the
sweetness up inside
To remember forever

Joan Wills

MY FIRST DAY AT SCHOOL

I remember that Monday morning,
My mother said to me,
'You're starting school today,'
I said 'Oh dear me.'

So I put my Sunday best dress on,
I must say I felt like a queen,
In my black clogs and thick woolly stockings,
And a pinny to keep my dress clean.

The time had come, we walked up the hill,
To the school they called St Peter's,
My mam held my hand but I wasn't scared,
Now I had to meet the teacher.

Then I sat at a desk and played with things,
There were lots of things to do.
I made some animals with plasticine,
And lots of funny men too.

The morning soon passed it was now twelve o'clock,
My sister took me by the hand,
Our mam had our dinners ready,
'Oh' I said 'I feel grand.'

I thought that's my first day in at school,
But I got quite a shock,
We had to go back in the afternoon,
School started again at one o'clock.

So back once again to the classroom,
Where we threaded wooden beads on string,
Then Mrs Holman played the piano,
She said we all had to stand up and sing.

The afternoon passed it had been a long day,
At least it seemed like it to me.
Although I enjoyed my first day at school
And to think I was only just three.

                    I am now 79.

N Stevenson

THE STREAM IN THE FOREST

A quiet misty morning by a stream
clear water flowing over stones
and the sound of birdsong
and the gentle dripping of leaves
misty mornings when the world
sleeps beyond the dawn, an intermission
within the world of nature

The peace and tranquillity in silence
wandering through a forest of green velvet
I become as one, with the owl
gliding silently amongst sylvan trees
of an ancient woodland
a beautiful owl winging his way
upon silent velvet-soft wings
silvered by moonlight
through the dark green velvet
of the forest of the night
accompanied by ancestral echoes of the past
the forest is for ever
part of our past, our present,
our future.

Brenda Straw

THE CLOUDS

Fleecy white clouds in a clear blue sky
Billowing and floating way up high
Sunshine streaming through patches of blue
Glorious green trees varying in hue . . .
Sweeping down hills, changing in view . . .
To the valleys of beauty

Natural scenes unfold in glory
As the coastline appears with another story
Of beauty untold and ever new
For eyes to behold and follow through
To a patchwork of fields with quaint villages between
Nestled and peaceful quite serene . . .
They bathe in their glory . . .

Mother Nature made the clouds in the sky
We accept them and never ask why
Or how the rain needs to fall
For all growing plants and trees so tall . . .
We take it all for granted
And yet we know that the rain is wanted . . .
For our needs in so many ways.

The Devonshire coast is the place to be
For beautiful sunsets reflected on shimmering sea . . .
As the sun, like an orange ball in the sky,
Slips below the horizon, as nightfall is nigh . . .
Rest for the weary at the end of the day.
We should be so thankful and learn to say
'Thanks be to God.'

A Joan Hambling

DERAILING THE GRAVY TRAIN

What's that sound, that splits the night?
What's that sound, that kills your sleep?

It must be me, and I'll be found
Caught in the searchlight's glare,
Kneeling by the side of the track,
At the point where there's no turning back,
From derailing the Gravy Train.

All the things that surround us,
All that we hold so dear,
Really stand for so little, or less,
When the moment of dawning draws near,
When the realisation of it becomes clear,
It's a fragile house of cards, built on fear.

Once, I used to ride the rails,
Now it feels that they ride me,
Or that I am clinging on, as it hurtles round the bend.
Now it seems I have to halt it,
Dead in its smoking tracks,
Before it thunders further, with more lost souls aboard.

I want to see this steaming beast
Lying helpless, panting and hissing, on its side.
Its carriages, now abandoned,
Collapse as if made of thin air.
There'll be others emerging, to survey the wreck,
Just like an ancient mariner, dancing on the deck.

Derailing the Gravy Train.

Richard Gould

THE LOWER YANGTZE

Swirling, winding,
 Twisting, grinding,
Through the gorges
 The river forges
Bubbling, foaming,
 Endlessly roaming,
Past the towns
 Of greys and browns,
Then free again
 Through fields of grain;
Past peasants toiling,
 Sunbaked, broiling;
Their sweat and strife
 Give them life.
The river, unheeding,
 Advancing, receding,
Sweeps along
 Powerful and strong,
Pushing to reach the sea
 Where it longs to be
Unbound and free.

Joan Boulton

FIELD WALKERS

We're out again walking the windy fields
under the wind-wiped Essex sky.
Each time-warped hedge and raw-boned tree
has its place deep in our own knotted grain,
such long-practised field walkers we.
Up on the muscular top of the land
in the bold clear light you can see for miles.
Far over there two others with their dog
share the great swathe, pin-small
but we know them well - all three.

Beguiled by the ever-changing scene
we rove free as air without any walls
and the walls in our minds swept clean away.
Though darkening clouds may come scudding in
and the wind be peppered with rain
we'll pull down our hats and keep right on
striding the old enduring ground
towards our horizons as long as we may.

David Poole

BECAUSE YOU WERE THERE

And then -
You were there.
With your voice
Fingering my collar,
Finding me
Guilty
As ever,
Of being
Myself.
And then the wind,
Letting your hair
Touch its occasional flames
On your shoulders.
I saw
All there
Coming to conjugate
As Present
Whatever it is
You do.
And Perfect,
Whoever it is
You are.

Kevin O'Keeffe

IN KIDGATE, LOUTH, IN AUTUMN

Doctors' surgery windows, that look down into
The car park behind Peter Rhodes, certainly see
                                    the autumn's revenue
Of harsh winds blowing into a well-trusted lee
At the Mercer Row end. The door's locked round about
Six o'clock, when people with shop jobs have come out
Driven home, and have left Louth town looking lonely.

Uncle, at the pawnshop, must have taken in pledge
Paintings, and ornaments, from the cottages here -
                                    then imagined a ledge
Of a window, regrettably clear;
And bare patches of brighter wallpaper.
Poverty was a cruel morale-scraper.
Favourite vases went to his shop with a tear.

Mornings are darker, when alarm clocks ring, or bleep.
Skies are mottled while weather decides what to do.
Once downstairs, a housewife takes her first furtive peep
Between curtains, desperate to obtain a clue . . .
Should the family take raincoats or go without?
It's no use taking risks, while storm clouds are about -
In the walk home with shopping, she could get wet through.

Gillian Fisher

EPIPHANY

With a young student teacher, blithely talking
About the aims of education -

While I can picture him hanging from a blackboard,
Crucified, as I was crucified.

Stan Downing

THE GROWING UP YEARS

Make the most of the growing up years
Join in the laughter share in the tears
Make the most of each hug and each kiss
There are the things you will really miss.
Make the most of the growing up years
Tell bedtime stories and quieten their fears
Share days at the seaside
And walks in the rain
Playing ball in the park
They many not come again
Those days don't last forever
They are gone all too soon
You cannot bring them back
Make life a joy, without gloom.
Those growing up years
You should love and enjoy
Spend time with your children
Each girl and each boy.
For the growing up years
Just go by so fast
And soon they are over
Lost way back in the past
Though you may share troubles
And shed many tears
They are all so worthwhile
In the growing up years.

M Pay-Watson

MINE

The only way I see you is looking from afar,
The only way I see you is to me a shining star,
I loved you from the moment you were put upon this earth.
I loved you the first day you walked upon this land,
I wished you could know how much I wanted to hold your tender
                                                    little hand,
I wanted you just to know I loved you and you to know you're mine,
But I know it cannot be until a later time,
I watched you grow into a woman,
So lovely and so good,
I wanted just to hold you,
Like a father should,
But I know this cannot be,
I just haven't got the time,
I will have to leave this world quite soon just knowing you are mine,
But I will always think of you from a lonely star,
And I will always love and watch over you because I know who you,
                        Really are.

P W Parker

A FACE IN THE CHERRY TREE

Could we have seen that day
A face in the cherry tree?
Dappled with light and shade
Leaves forming a smile for me?

Recalled like a long-lost ghost
From memories' deep alleyways
Beheld some forgotten scene
Of old times and yesterdays.

Laughter carried by the breeze
Songs of birds and honeybee
Humming summer full a'bloom
Enhancing such fantasy.

Could we have seen that face
Or were our wits deceived?
Can fancy change our world
With mysteries unbelieved?

Patricia Battell

THE MOORS

The road twines and curls upwards
From lush pastures to peaks unseen.
High sentinel hedges hide their secrets
From the searching eye,
Until suddenly they cease,
Halted by nature's night-cold line
Of invisible barriers.

Revealed, majestic moors' purple-pillar
The clouds which water them
Like a herd of tethered dinosaurs
With mauve, green brands,
Slack mouths dribbling water in rivulets
To trampled bogs beneath
Their massive feet.

Sheep flocks and pony herds scatter
Their backs, converging and multiplying,
Sucking sustenance and sanctuary,
Seasoning with mists.
Stone warts in circles cling unchanged
By centuries of wearing wind
And winter rain.

Sandra Lewis

THE SILVER BIRCH

Goodbye old tree
Your time has come.
You will be missed
Not only by the winged ones,
You, who stood above the view
Of newer folk and houses too.
I did but know you fleetingly
But those old branches made a song
With every breeze,
That told of long ago
And open space
Before the scrambling human race
Hummed to and fro beneath your glance.
You leave us sad.
No silhouette to grace the sky,
Knowing that time stands not still
And wonder.

B Margaret Rose

AS I GO ON

As I continue to grow older each day,
I grow stronger and gently start to break away
From whatever I feel is holding me back
It's hard enough to go on and be strong
When I lack -
The energy and drive to fulfil my dreams,
Or just do well in life and be comfortable it seems,
That wherever I go in life there will be -
A hurdle standing in front of me.
But I won't let it stop me
And each time you'll see
Emerging a stronger and wiser me!

Joleen McPartland

IF TIME WAS A PLACE

If time was a place, where would it end?
The journey of life what joys would it send, life is like dream of hopes
and truths stay in this time with me my dear,
together forever untouched so clear, motion in space, eternity of pain.
Are we all one, in this never ending game.
Is one and only or why the shame,
to be born to be loved only by name.

Test the same love plays a part in the life we start
but if time was a place,
remember these words,
inspired and new like love itself tender and cared treat it with care,
precious and new if time was a place?
Where 'did we dream'.

Gill Robson

JUST FOR DAD

(Written in memory of Kenneth Terrence Roper, my dad)

This one is for Dad,
He showed me right from wrong.
This is just for Dad,
His love forever strong.

This one is for Dad,
The best friend I ever had.
This is just for Dad,
For his love we should be glad.

This one is for Dad,
Who, to us all, was dear.
This is just for Dad,
His presence always near.

Deanna Lorraine Dixon

THE COUNTRYMAN

The Countryman begins to sing
His thoughts are of the coming spring
He sees the signs those shoots of green
With winter passed, the worst he's seen

The cuckoo comes and swallows soon
And countryside gets into June
Dawn chorus' welcome in the morn'
He's feeling good, glad he was born

Moorhen builds her nest upon the stream
Everywhere is like a dream
Mowing grass to make the hay
As sun shines on another day

The Countryman enjoys the life
He shares it with his darling wife
The seed is sown, away the plough
He's thinking of the summer now

Raymond J Hobbs

LOVE

Teardrops are golden like the first dawn
Encircled in life that must journey on
Temple of light from a daughter to a wife
Learning so much through a happy sad life
Echoes flow down through the mixed coloured line
Proclaiming to me that you were once mine
A broken promise lies bleeding forever in time
Our love bruised and battered though never quite shattered
Love binds us as one as life journeys on
Laced through the lives of our daughters and our sons

Katherine Kennedy Quaye

MY LORD, MY KING

My Lord, my King,
Your love has saved me
From the despair that was within,
Destroying my living soul.
So desolate was I.
Neglecting my faith, neglecting all.
Yet, you still loved me.
Still held out your arms in compassion.
Comforted me in my need.
Held me like a child.
You guided me back,
You watched over me.
Then sent me your Spirit,
To fill into me
Your love and forgiveness.
For that, you died for me.
My Lord, my King.

Zoë Fail

CRADLE SONG

Crafted out of memories
Fashioned from our past
Engraved within our hearts
Every dream lasts
Moulded from security
Woven with our love
Stitched with pure perfection
Fitted like a glove
Created in a moment
Protected from then on
A work of art presented
The circle of life goes on.

D Finkel

BERYL'S NEW DRESS

'Wonderful,' the shop girl oozed;
'It was made for you,' another cooed.
Naggings of doubt grew on Beryl,
'You'll miss this bargain at your peril.'
Still undecided, she 'Ummed' and 'Aahed'
And stripped off again down to her bra.

'I'll try the blue again,' she said
So the assistant pulled it over her head.
'Fine, Madam,' the girl replied with a sneer
For the other dress was twice as dear.
'If you don't mind, I'll let my husband see.'
'Do as you wish, it's not up to me.'

Boredom now was setting in
On the shop-girl who was tall and thin
And could wear anything she ever saw
Because she didn't sag right down to the floor.
This customer was becoming quite a pain,
Any commission she'd get wasn't worth the gain.

Soon Beryl returned, wreathed in smiles,
'He thinks the blue is better by miles'
She said, happily changing again
And breathing out, with relief from the pain.
The assistant nodded and left Beryl alone.
Now all she had to do was find a 'phone.

Ringing her son from the station in Reading,
Beryl exclaimed over her dress for the wedding.
Then she enquired what the bride's mother would wear,
Asking after the colour as if she hadn't a care.
When asked before, they hadn't a clue;
'Yes, now we know.' The answer was *blue!*

K E Smith

EGG

You are involved with murder. No
innocence has slaughtered me;
my juices, chromed and weeping,
remain a birth into appetite, a
temporary life in the world's
round tin, a purgatory of water.
No Baptist am I.

No ranter, absorbed in your mannish
shorthand of hunger; I am a small
pale berry in a cracked shell -
fruit of clucking vine. In an atom-breath,
my toupee sliced, my soul paranoid
under the judgement spoon, I have
only the dumb insolence of an egg.

I am Egg, the seed of eaters.
My Pentecost is fire. In my prophetic
time I am the egg in prayer -
I am Kafka. O Man, whose shell will
thicken in the earth limes, his hunger
in the weed, consider: egg has the
world's shape,

The spherical 'O' of an abortion
- my soft whites a prayer.
I am the birth before hunger,
a mini-world sleighted against your
veto - or the regular breakfast kin.
Man the world-maker eats of life.
Look on my yoke and despair:

It is the egg's revenge.

Simon Richardson

MOTHER'S RUIN

I can see that glimmer of hope fade from your eye
As yet again your patience is tried
That expression of a mother's love for her wayward child
Has peaked then ebbed and finally died
I've seen you pushed and crushed for far too long
But his hold on you is so terribly strong
He invades your happiness with his own selfish ways
But it only reminds father of his own youthful days
You pretend you are weak but you really are strong
As he strays from the right path onto the wrong
You brought him into this world your own bundle of joy
And who would have thought he'd still be a boy
Oh when will he stand on his own two feet?
So that you now may take a leisurely back seat
You've had your fill of anxious black nights
Loud knocks at the door giving you frights
But I've seen you pick up the pieces time after time
If you hadn't I'm sure a real life of crime
And how many times must you bail the lad out
Has he really no idea what life is about
Now mothers are mothers invisible bonds you have tied
As he comes back to your apron it's a great place to hide
But with that sixth sense of yours you know trouble's brewing
Oh that beastly brother of mine will be my mother's ruin.

Michael Bellerby

WRITER'S BLOCK

As I stand here slowly thinking
Of a thought that I could think of
Then a thought pops into question
What was I just thinking of?

Then will I when or won't I never
Catch a thought and pin it down
As I stand here slowly thinking
Do thoughts make a thinking sound?

Richard Priest

MY BED

The best place on Earth to me is my bed,
It feels so welcome as I lay down my head
To rest myself from the cares of the day
And thank the Lord as I lay and pray.

Ideas and inspirations flood into my head
Reliving memories as I lay in my bed.
Both my babies were born in this bed, what joy!
Later a girl, but first a boy.

The sweet dreams I dream as I drift away
Make a playground for fantasies at the end of the day.
The drifting off to a deep slumber of sleep
Helps one hold onto the secrets you keep.

When I awake to a brand new day
'Thank the Lord for a good night's rest' I say,
Reluctant to rise and leave my haven of peace
And all the thoughts my bed helps me to release.

But rise I must to face what the day holds in store,
Be it workload or leisure and what is more
We know whatever it holds, at the end of the day
We will find our repose as in our beds we lay.

In all the world my bed is best,
I love my bed, it gives me rest.

Joyce Hammond

WINTER'S LITTLE CREATURES

Snow lay thick on the ground,
Little creatures asleep all around.
No little creature stirred,
Just wrapped up warm in his fur.

The sun rose at dawn,
The first woodland creature gave a yawn.
This is meant to be the start of spring,
But no birds wanted to sing.

Winter was usually over, this year it was late,
Little creatures in the wood started to wake.
Dens to mend, fix that nest,
Some of the birds thought of the flight west.

They were upset as disturbed from their sleep,
They will need to tread carefully, the snow lies deep.
They leave behind little paw prints,
The glare off the snow gives a strange light tint.

Two big brown eyes out of a den peep,
Awake from their winter's sleep,
Unsteady on those furry feet,
Old friends to find and meet.

L M Britton

BEDRUTHAN STEPS, CORNWALL

Above Bedruthan's craggy heights
On thermal winds a buzzard soars
With wide-stretched wings and raking claws
Drops like a stone, its prey to smite
Unwary creatures, slow in flight
So vulnerable on the grassy floor
Heed well the rook, its warning 'caw'
Venture forth only 'neath the mantle of night

Bedruthan Steps, such a perilous place
Where menacing cliffs rear high to the skies
Precipitous steps, so treacherous and steep
To these beckoning dangers turn a questioning face
Such bright sparkling surf an innocence belies
And tempts to deceive . . . take care lest ye weep!

Francis Sawyer

DESTINY

With youth's exuberance and confident style,
We fearlessly tread the unknown mile.
Do we choose the road ahead,
Or are with unseen guidance led?

For fame and fortune should we aspire
Or be content on a lesser spire.
To mingle in nondescript enclosures
Or reach for eminent exposures.

Friends made and lost along the way,
Only staunch friendships are sure to stay.
Such faults and imperfections excused
A mutual interchange freely used.

As seasons pass with relentless speed
The chance to reach own goals recede.
In fervent youth - our notions soar
With fair opportunities - will score.

Our aspirations finally spent,
With small achievement must be content.
Life's journey ends like a transient dream,
A moment of time in eternity.

Joy M Jordan

SORROW

We're still waiting
for you to call
as you did
to chat and that
have a bit of fun
and now
the race is run
your journey's done
We knew that you
were ill and
very brave to
carry on
and now you're gone
we're pleased you
were our friend
but now the end
You never said
that you'd be dead
and we're still
          waiting . . .

Connie Moseley

AN INDIAN

An Indian sitting on the top of a hill
His horse standing there so still
Indian with his colourful head-dress
Stroking his horse with tenderness
Sitting Bull, with his head held high
Bow and arrow pointing towards the sky.

Behind him I can see his braves
Soldiers that fought them in their graves
Fighting for their precious land
Together the Indians stand.

His squaw sitting in the tepee
With his son upon her knee
Now he comes home, his son to see
How his eyes light up, fills him with glee.

Now all the Indians ride the plains
Old Sitting Bull, so proudly reigns
Won his battle, won the day
His braves behind him all the way.

B W Jones

THE CUSHY NUMBER

Miss Simpson was her name,
Oh, that was our art teacher,
I'll just put you in the frame,
We'd all sit in her class on a Friday morning,
Fidgeting and moaning,
All of us yawning,
I only picked art because,
I thought it a cushy number,
But oh, what a blunder!
It was OK for homework you see,
Because I always got my brother to do it for me,
But then exam time came around,
That's when she really found
The truth behind my scam and
That it had all been a sham,
I went from A+ to C- all in one day,
But hold on, it was OK,
It wasn't all that bad,
You can guess what fun we'd really had,
Sitting in the corner seat,
Eating cheese and pickle sandwiches,
Now that certainly was a treat.

Sally Hunter

TRUE LOVE

True love is like a strong forged chain
Withstanding every strain
Linking those in willing bonds
In sunshine or in rain

No force can cause this chain to break,
No circumstances of life
Can cause a love forged chain to snap,
Thus parting man and wife

A marriage based on love, not lust
Will stand the test of years,
The bonds of true love will not part,
Nor marriage end in tears

Respect, integrity and care
Are links in loves strong chain,
Forgiveness too and tolerance
Will withstand every strain

The strength of every chain is said
To be it's weakest link,
But burdens shared in every part
Are stronger than you'd think

True love is not like slavery
Restricting every move,
But, two in harness sharing all,
Such are the bonds of love

Horace Hartley

TRYING TIMES

No time for me to try to write
My trying times last through 'til night.
I try with rhymes and subjects new
But the verses I get, come just from you.
'Where's my socks that I can't find
Where's my shirt I'm all behind
Where's my breakfast and cup of tea?'
'Sorry darling I'm writing poetry!'
'But the kids are screaming in the hall
No wonder you don't hear me when I call.
Now the car won't start, ring a cab for me'
'Sorry darling, I'm writing poetry!'
'But the weather's bad and getting worse.'
'Alright darling, just one more verse!'
'But the kids aren't dressed and still playing the fool
Come now children, time for school.
I'm off to work, won't be back this time.'
'OK darling just one more line.'
The postman's knocking on the door
The puppy's puddles on the floor
The phone keeps ringing, now what was said?
How can I concentrate with all these rhymes
Going through my head
'It's your husband calling,
I won't be back this century!
So you can write as much as you like of that damn poetry!'
I am distraught, but there's another rhyme!
I'll write it down, just one more time.

Constance I Roper

SILENCE THAT WE WEEP

The seeds of life run so deep,
No-one hears the silence that we weep.
The day, the nights feel so long,
The essence of love, present and strong.
Look around us and see our friends,
Simple words, that broken fences mend.
But as they breathe heavy in their sleep,
They don't hear the silence that we weep.

My love, their face on my mind I keep,
Do not hear the silence that I weep.
The children playing all day long,
The bustling streets the market throng.
They have no idea of what I feel,
My outer layers, bare and peeled.
They follow each other like lambs to sheep,
They do not hear the silence that I weep.

Now I have learned, with all my heart,
As people pass, and lovers part.
Only time can heal, and years can reap,
To ease this silence that I weep.

Dawn Graham

MARKET THOUGHTS

Why must the stallholder randomly scatter
Apostrophes over the goods he displays?
Useless and ugly they carelessly spatter
The labels in most of his baskets and trays.
We'll all buy the wares he sells by his patter,
But please put an end to this maddening craze!

Grahame Godsmark

CANINE FANTASY

I am a dog. We come in all shapes and sizes.
Some are all scruffy, some win the best prizes.

Some are very good, some, very very bad,
But 'I' am the very best you ever had.

Loving you, is what I do best.
Asleep on your lap, both at rest.

But when we awake, my lead in your hand,
It becomes to me a wonderland.

Running down the country lane,
Familiar sights and smells again.

Just a moment, this new scent on the floor.
I think it's someone you knew before.

A lady's hat, and dressed in blue,
I can tell by your manner, she is special to you.

We can tell each other's needs,
And listen to each other's pleads.

I can tell when you are sad
Or happy and when you feel glad.

Then they say, dogs can't talk!
Just ask me, 'Want a walk?'

So ask that lady dressed in blue,
If she would like to marry you.

For she has a small French poodle
Just right for me to *ca-noodle!*

Herbert Ronald Robson

WHY?

Why are some of us thin and some of us fat?
Why are we not content with this and that?

Why do we want to travel to foreign shores?
Why do we go on those strange mystery tours?

Why don't we complain when things aren't right
Why do we grumble and mutter and get uptight?

Why do we moan about the weather every single day?
Why is it nearly always the first thing we say?

Why can't we feel the earth spinning around?
Why do we say our feet are firmly on the ground?

Why do we say 'no' when we really mean 'yes'?
Why? I don't know but I suppose I could guess!

Why? Why? Why? Must have gone down in history.
Why? Because it's one of life's little mysteries!

Barbara D Price

BINGO

It's Sunday night and it's Bingo time the
hall is packed to the brim, lots of ageing
plump ladies with tall skinny partner all
wanting a chance just to win.

As the caller gets ready the hall lights are
lowered the tension it starts to flood out,
those ageing plump ladies with tops off
their pencils are waiting there turn just to shout.

When Bingo is called there are looks that could
kill from the players that go every week,
your life's on the line if you win lots of money,
keep your head down you don't dare to speak.

When the night's nearly over and they haven't
won again, they vow they won't go anymore,
but next week in the hall it will be full of
ageing plump ladies playing Bingo waiting
their chance just to call.

Sue Curtis

SOUL-SEARCHING

She stands all forlorn looking out to the sea
In a daze she is pondering of what is to be
The peace and the quiet help her thoughts to express
Her feelings of fear and of dark emptiness
Of what will become of her life from here on
And if she has strength to continue as one
The pain that is felt is too great to endure
The blue of the sea is so totally pure
To end it all now would be simple and sweet
Knowing forever that her life's incomplete
But suddenly there on the horizon afar
In the dusk of the night there appears a bright star
It twinkles and shines on the waves of the deep
And makes her heart flutter and wanting to weep
She realises then that life has its pleasure
And there are many things left to want and to treasure
With a sprint in her walk she turns from the shore
And hurries on home to start life once more.

Leila Caryll

FORWARD AND BACK IN TIME

I've walked into your bar, the fire a lovely big glow
Menus standing in a row, neatly printed without a bow
Long ago, so I'm told, 1860 carriages at your door
I've missed the carriages but cars are standing in a long row.
Moustache and beard, King George, you've appeared staring
Imprinted forever within that long mirror so grand
Toby jugs on shelves so high, sitting as if to wonder why
Hunting horn, horse brasses, hanging wall lights shining bright
To my eyes' delight, sparkling bottles for all to see.

I treasure that moment in front of your log fire,
For my journey will be long and time will bring me back to you
To that coast I'll travel and on my boat I'll be
Out on that winter's rough North Sea
And wonder if thee will be with me.
I'm now trying to think of some lines to write of that
                                   coffee drinking and strife
Ah, I hear a bark and a growl, that's Brandy the Alsatian dog
Italian proprietor, face shining so bright
Two tickets he's handed, a choice that's for me
I've chosen my ticket that one on the left
Dinner at night it be so fine, come lunch time the next day,
                                   you'll be mine
Glowing, glowing, your log fire whilst I listen to that midnight beat.

Peeping through your window I spy proprietor JJ
Who's writing the menu of the day
The Queen and Prince Charles have lunched inside and shalt I
Now I'm here once more standing at your door.
Guest on Wednesday bags all packed in your corridor
Aeroplane pictures lists of missions of long ago
466 bombardment troup commenced activities August 1st, 1943
Their last mission so long ago twenty-fifth April 1945
The crew of Laden Maid 786th Squadron pilot captain
                                   George T Zeigler.

I stepped inside to treasure that moment in front of your coalfire
For I've only my electric fire
Polished tables and Dralon-backed chairs neatly stood
A customer stares so hard and long, perhaps she'll sing a song
Or I wonder was there something wrong
For two old ladies that had been staying, a gine and tonic order
                                                   of that day
Pub garden for summer drinks all upon wooden seats I'll sit
Red sports car just a star I'll never meet zooming to that village
                                                   green
And I'll remember those treasured moments in front of log fire.

K Latham

THE MISSING SEAT

It was a beautiful day,
I sat on the seat, by the sea front,
To enjoy the sun, it was such a treat,
To watch the ships,
Then along came a little lady,
She came straight for me.
Have you seen my seat?
Such a lovely one,
For it was sheltered from the wind,
Yet in the sun,
I cannot find it anywhere,
Oh, I replied, maybe
It's behind the bend,
Or taken to mend.
But looking at her I felt,
Perhaps she was lost,
Maybe all she wanted
Was to talk to me.

Nancy Edwards

THE DOME

Blackpool has its tower,
Great Yarmouth has its pier.
Cleethorpes - miles of golden sand
Newquay's a surfer's paradise
       huge waves roll in there.

There's Brighton and Eastbourne
With their chalk cliffs rising high
Then there's Dover, lovely Dover,
Where the white cliffs nearly reach the sky.

We have Grimsby with its fishing smacks
And Boston with its docks,
Follow the waters in Norfolk
Find the rivers, lakes and locks.

In Wales there are beaches with unpronounceable names
With coves and caves and little bays
Only reached by sandy lanes.

There is Morecambe Bay in Cumbria
If you take the western coast
150 square miles of water
Which recedes, so the natives boast
To leave a vast expanse of golden sand
On this north-western coast.

You may ask where this is leading to
This saga of beach and coast
The point of it all is *Ingoldmells*
Ingoldmells is my home
And its only claim to fame so far
'*Is that dam great dome*'.

Ruby Doughty

ONCE OUR ENGLAND

Had nothing but cuts
For a long time
Just when I thought everything
Was fine
Then up came Brussels from
Nowhere I note
They are trying to dominate
Us without even one vote
Who gave them permission
To rule our land?
Why should we give them
Everything to hand?
We want our country
To stay free
The way our older people
Want it to be
They'll try to make us pay
Taxes far too high
And put their big statues
Not wanted up to the sky
But we should stop it
Before it begins
And make sure
That our England wins
Stay free England for all time
This country is not theirs
This country once was mine.

Velma Winstanley

THOUGHTS

Honeybees live in hives,
From the honeypots we eat.
Policemen always on the beat,
Tired and heavy must be their feet.
Strawberry jam comes in jars,
Some more exotic from afar.
Fires burning, logs a'glowing,
Snow falling from the icy air a'blowing.
Footprints and handprints in the sand,
Children playing in a band.
Rain pouring from the sky
Always makes the people sigh.
Autumn leaves a'falling
I think I have a calling
To end this poem, and say *Goodbye!*

Joy Sharp

AUTUMN SLEEPER

Deep, deep and even deeper
Into the mind of the autumn sleeper
Summer's gone and winter beckons
Spring soon or so she reckons
But changes come with the years
Different face, different fears
Still she looks as only she can
In her endless search for that perfect man
Where will she find him, how will she know
She'd best hurry up before it's time to go
But nothing changes except the lies
Same old endings, just different guys
Wish her luck, hope she'll soon be free
When finally she knows what the rest of us see

Douglas Lawrie

WITCHES' CHANT

Round the cauldron we must go,
Adding entries we must throw.
Throw in eggs of wild birds,
Plus the brains of computer nerds.
Turn a toad inside out,
The scrape it so his guts fall out.

Stir, stir, stir the cauldron,
Bubble, bubble, bubble cauldron.

Tail of rat and nose of dog,
Eyes of newt and toes of frog.
Teeth of vampire, bat and human leg,
One child's nail plus one rotten chicken's egg.
Stir and do a sin,
Then add a firework to make a din.

Stir, stir, stir the cauldron,
Bubble, bubble, bubble cauldron.

Add a tooth from a crocodile's snap,
Then the hamster who has taken a nap.
Just to make this smell nice,
Add a clove of garlic sliced.
Add the slime from a pond,
Then a wave from my magic wand.

Stir, stir, stir the cauldron,
Bubble, bubble, bubble cauldron.

Then just to round this all off,
Add the toe that I've just cut off.

Ah ha ha ha ha!

Katie Hocking (12)

WALKING ON AIR

From the depths of despair
I now feel like I'm walking on air,
A year ago I was in great pain
And I hope I never go through that again,
It appears I had a large blood clot in my leg
And it felt like my vein was blocked by an egg,
Eight days in hospital I had to spend
I thought that the pain would never end,
With injections and a load of tablets too
They were thinning my blood to let it get through,
Now I've had tests done to find out the cause
And for a while from Warfarin tablets I had to pause,
Now they've found out what they needed to know
I'm back on the tablets for life because they say so,
Because if I don't take my Warfarin tablets once again
I'm going to keep getting clots and lots more pain,
But now after a year has gone so fast
The problem of blood clots is a thing of the past,
Right now I feel wonderful and alive
And pleased that *God* has let me survive,
I've a penfriend Irene who's helped me too
Sending me lovely letters which I've had to reply to,
Writing letters and talking on the phone
Has helped build me up and not feel alone,
Sometimes the nights seems so long and unfair
But knowing there are loving people who really care,
Is a wonderful thing that fills me with joy
And I can never be alone with friendships to enjoy,
So from feeling down in the dumps and full of despair
It really does feel like I'm walking on air!

George Reed

SEASONS OF A KENTISH LIFE

When Winter has finally done its worst,
And the earth lies hard beneath snow,
We look to the Springtime to cheer our hearts,
To the Spring God has promised, we know,
For changelessly, yearly He gives the earth warmth
And sunshine, to make all things grow.

Comes Summer next with its hot sunny days,
Gentle breezes and soft-falling rain,
Bright-coloured flowers and tall-standing trees
All Earth is alive once again.
Short is the season, such beauty must wither
And only its memories remain.

Creeps in the Autumn, silently, hazily,
Leaves change to scarlet and yellow.
We harvest the fruits of our labours under
Sun mild and misty, and mellow.
We till the soil for next year; chills the wind,
Winter waits; and once more we'll have snow.

Each warm arising from the frozen earth
Each new strength building from another birth
Has grown from all the years gone by and past.
High summer in our hearts must fade away
Replaced by colder bleaker slopes to climb
With courage drawn from those who toiled before.

The seasons of life pass,
And only memory can still the petals of past summers strew,
Yet still we strive towards the Eastern Sun whose warmth is ever new.

Phyllis, Valerie and Helen Marsh
(Three generations of a Kentish family)

FLIGHT OF THE SWALLOW

Swirling sands on the winds of time
Swallow in flight - stars that shine
ever bright - souls to unite.
From the plateau of passion quench
the thirst,
Drink well of the wine
Beloved Sahara sister of mine.
For deep is the ocean and far is the land
where memories linger hand-in-hand.
Surrender the spirit from that which yearns
release the heart from the fire that burns.
How great is the pleasure?
How perfect the pain?
A lesson of love, giving to gain, this single
grain that travels by night,
Transcending all matter into the light.
Deep into the void no more to dream
So gentle this spirit in cosmic stream.

A Lucas

OUR HAVEN

Why did we come to this corner of England?
To the peace and quiet of this village in Devon?
We searched around from north, south, east and west,
Until at last we found the best,
A real haven from the worry and strife,
And the noisy bustle of city life.

We came from London to the pure air of Devon,
And thought we had really reached our heaven
With the rolling hills and gentle vales,
Despite the rain and the fearsome gales.

The hills, the valleys, the moors, the sea,
All these are perfect heaven to me.
By the quiet ripple of a moorland stream
Is where we like to sit and dream,
Not of the past so far away,
But where next shall we go on a lovely day?

Muriel Johnson

GOREDALE BECK

Janet's foss
The mighty force
Of water
Steeply falling
Into the pool
Swirling and splashing
Over the stones

An uneven path
Winding and wet
Alongside
Swiftly flowing
Goredale Beck
Running towards
The river Aire.

On we go
Leaving the stream
To unite
With Malham Beck
Lower down.
We bestride
The Pennine Way.

Lisa Wolfe

THE PATTERN OF LIFE

The pattern of life is a mystery to me
Although it's laid out for all to see
From the day we are born it begins to unfold
It's something intangible - nothing to hold
Each pattern is different - there's a reason why
But you try to find it - or change it - you won't,
      so don't try.

As for the colour it varies from day to day
Ranging from gold-blue and often grey
This depends mainly on events of life
For some the pattern is dulled by strife
Others find patches of gold here and there
To hope for perfection is more than one dare.

As we grow older the edges start fraying
And for some unknown reason find ourselves praying
For help that it will hold out just a little longer
Many use willpower - a certainty to make it stronger

So if in your travels you come across a pattern or two
That seem to need brightening - stop - and see
      what you can do
Don't hesitate or think it's absurd
May need only a smile or even a word
For although it's a mystery - I'm fully aware
To keep it alive - needs loving and care.

Eleanor Smithers

DISUNITY

Red white and blue the Union flag flies
For patriotic Brits it's reaching the skies.
But resounding rumblings round this pleasant land,
That a break-up threatens this happy band.

For this happy Union there's a wonderful story.
Over hundreds of years covered in glory.
Against the odds the Brits have been victorious,
Tales of great bravery they have been glorious.

Threats of a break-up leaves a dark cloud,
Losing our traditions that makes us all proud.
The cost of disunity with danger is fraught,
Keeping us united needs wisdom and thought.

Separation seems the Union's infection,
A split of the Union is a wanton deflection.
Being insular and not united,
With the possibility of a break-up we are being blighted.

We must keep the Union before it is lost,
With four little provinces what is the cost.
Keeping continuity a clarion call.
United we stand, divided we fall.

Robert Baslington

FAMILY

I have family
My brother, my sister, Mum and Dad
They make me so happy, even glad
They are there to listen to me
And I am there when they need me
So it is important that I have family.

E Perfect

WINNERS AND LOSERS

Your troubles are over
You have money enough
To buy anything and do
Your own stuff

Your car is expensive
Your house very large
And all that you want
Can be put on a charge

Holidays anywhere
For as long as you like
No more travelling on
Your dad's worn out bike

No more worrying
About debts you've not paid
Or forgetting how long it was
Since last you got laid

You can dress all your ladies
With clothes you endorse
And all kinds of jewels
To go with them of course

Friends you have plenty
The old ones you've shed
When you had them you
Sucked them dry
And now they are bled

Your troubles are over
I wish you well from the heart
Although it upset me
When we had to part

I'm one of your old friends
One of the few
When you came into money
You told us to shoo

I remember the old days
When you were nice
When the strength of our friendship
Did not have a price

You walk in different circles now
And follow the current trend
You might have won some money
But I have lost a friend.

James Valentine Sullivan

PAST TENSE

There stood Robert the Bruce and his trusty spider,
With Jean McGregor and her child beside her,
And William Wallace wanting no hassle,
As they made their way to Edinburgh Castle,
The Scots wha hae where Wallace bled,
And chronicles of this are often read,
The timorous beastie by Robert Burns,
Gave nation upon nation a mighty turn,
Those Scots of the past in blazing glory,
And fights with the English were often gory.
But time has settled amidst the dust,
With Clans accepting this as a must,
The MacDonalds, the McLeods and McDuff,
The McStays, the McPhersons have had enough,
To live in peace and settle the score,
And to make friends with forever more.

William D Watt

JUST LIKE MAGIC

I went into my garden to plant bulbs in a row,
Daffodils and tulips, I didn't really know,
They slept all through the winter and when the sunshine came,
Green stalks appeared like magic but they all looked the same.

Then just like magic,
The heads all opened up before my eyes,
Just like magic,
In yellow, pink and red to my surprise.
Just like magic,
My garden there in colour was alive,
Just like magic, it was magic.

I searched among my lettuce leaves, what do you think I found?
A furry caterpillar lying on the ground.
I thought I'd found a buddy, at last I had a friend,
How could I know by summer our friendship had to end?

Then just like magic,
My furry friend became a butterfly,
Just like magic,
With coloured wings it headed for the sky.
Just like magic,
I cannot figure out the reason why,
It was magic, purely magic.

Just like magic
The ugly duckling changed into a swan.
Just like magic,
The darkest night becomes the brightest dawn.
Just like magic,
A rainbow's colours just go on and on,
Just like magic, it was magic.

P A Kelly

BOSNIAN CHILD

What do you see little Bosnian child?
War and starvation
Running rife, running wild
What do you see
Through your veiled eyes of tears?
Enough wreckage and ruin
To last all your years?
Tell me dear child, what can you see
Your loved ones no more, no family
No one to help you now you are alone
Stuck in an orphanage
That is now your home
No one to love you, no one to care
No father or mother to visit you there
No sisters or brothers you can depend on
Starved now of affection
Since they all passed on
Scant food in your stomach
Not enough to share around
No childish laughter, you make not a sound
You rock in your cot, your blanket a rag
Hands tied to your cot sides
Mouth wearing a gag
But hope will soon flicker
And grow day by day
For help is soon coming, child, down your way
Then you will see things happen
Like never before
As soon as our helpers arrive at your door
God bless you my child, may peace and happiness reign
And may you not suffer, not ever again.

Eleanor Dunn

FROM BYWAYS TO HIGHWAYS

Have you got a favourite beauty spot,
That you drive to on those days,
When you fancy peace and quiet in leafy green byways?

There are lovely views to look at,
You can park just where you wish,
And you know a secret hidden pool that simply teems with fish.

You've been going there for years,
And the neighbouring village pub,
Serves a special home-brewed beer with its special home-made grub.

It's a place to go in springtime,
When the trees are bursting green,
And the fresh pale yellow primrose transforms the roadside scene.

You go there in the summer,
When the hotness of the day,
Is diminished by the shadows that lie thick along your way.

And you've been there in the autumn,
When the leaves on every tree,
Have a brown and golden beauty that you never tire to see.

You've been there in the winter,
When the snow that hides the ground,
Lies thick and freshly white and can be seen for miles around.

Have you been down that way lately?
It's quite different now you know,
Your heaven's now a hell on earth - the planners had a go.

Your lane's a bare and straight highway,
A motorway it feeds,
The pub's changed hands and now a caff supplies the masses' needs.

Why must the planners lay down roads,
To rush us all non-stop,
Straight through the very places where we'd much prefer to stop?

Stephen R Ramsden

GROWING OLD

I see them sitting
All alone
Their faces set
Like jagged stone
No thoughts I think
Are in their head
Just dreams for them
Inside their bed
No passion, joy
Just memories there
Hearts still beating
Souls so bare
Sometimes a movement
Slow unsure
Their lives ebbing
They feel no more
They sit like statues
And hope for death
Their bodies crave
That final breath
Their eyes so full
With sadness and pain
In God they trust
I hope not in vain.

J Brooks

THE QUAY

High up on the quay
Overlooking the waves
Stands a girl with a son
Just like you and me

Just like you and me
Holding hands together
Before you went to sea
In your pride and joy

In your pride and joy
You sailed away
Never to return
For ever and a day

For ever and a day
I will wait in vain
Hoping you will return
Hoping to see you again

Hoping to see you again
I look out to sea
But there is only driftwood
Where your ship used to be

Where your ship used to be
Now stands an empty berth
As a reminder to me
I will soon give birth

I will soon give birth
My only salvation
In this lonely life
My only vocation

My only vocation
Looking out to sea
Standing with my son
High up on the quay.

S A Kay

INCOME SUPPORT

Income Support is anything but.
Have you been in a social rut?
Makes you squirm in every fibre,
Trying to hide up your own lurid Kyber.
I don't smoke, and hardly drink.
More frugal a life you cannot think.
Can't buy games for Harriet,
Or spray to rid fleas off the cat.
Can't afford make-up or a face-lift.
As for a hair-do? I'm scuppered, I'm miffed.
I dream of slithering 'tween silken sheets,
Or to sit in a window seat reading Keats.
Neck and lobes dripping with gold,
Sniffing Chardonnay, sipping champagne sparkling cold.
You can't dispute that we are thrifty,
But there's no jobs there when you are fifty!
We're both workers, haven't we proved?
But those DSS clerks stay unmoved.
Take me away from nicotine stained halls
And those impersonally numbered intercom calls,
And all the signs of rampant poverty!
Alright don't give me money, but
Please leave me my dignity!
Don't want your money, I want a job!
Give me a chance to be a snob!

A Van Den Tooren

THE ELM TREE

Now that it has gone,
our whole view has changed.
We had always admired its permanence,
its solitary sturdiness.
When we returned after visiting her;
She had of course been talking
about the elm, those interlocked initials.
She would never say, never tell us
who carved them, who RJ was.
The men from the Council had been,
'It has to go' they said, 'Dutch elm disease.'
Now Leylandi forms a green wall,
impregnable, meaningless.
From a small branch, I carved enjoined lovers,
but now, as the wood dried out, it has split,
and the lovers have parted.
They are high on the top shelf,
in the dark of the cupboard
under the stairs.

Robert E Fairclough

MY PICTURE OF SCOTLAND

The beautiful Highlands of Scotland
Is like a picture with no compare
You can catch the sight of an eagle
As it floats on a thermal of air.

With sheep grazing all around hillside
And a stream rippling down through the glen
Away in the distance a ruin
All that's left of an old but 'n' ben.

On the hillside at point of advantage
Near the ruins of the old but 'n' ben
With antlers held aloft proudly
Stands the monarch of the glen.

You can hear the song of a skylark
As it hovers way up above
With the scent that comes from the heather
Completes my picture of the Scotland I love.

D Parley

BIG DEAL

Throughout it all you were no more than a friend;
Our hearts weren't involved and we didn't pretend,
And we used to take turns in acting the flirt:
I thought 'no strings attached' would save me from hurt.
And because I had nothing better to do
It was carefree and fun to spend time with you.

But in spite of myself I started to care;
Being apart from you was too much to bear,
Then when you wanted out, my heart filled with grief
'Though I told you my sighs were sighs of relief.
You'd fallen in love with your soon-to-be-wife:
I forced a smile and wished you, 'Have a nice life.'

Yet after all this time you're still in my head:
Do you think of me while you're sharing her bed?
I *know* I have no right to feel this much pain,
But why didn't you love me, I ask again;
That's the question which haunts me down through the years -
My eyes were wide open, but still sting with tears.

Kim Latham

EARLY SUMMER

Early summer is not complete
Without the 'wheep, wheep' of the peewit
Complaining of my presence
And breaking the quiet
Of the sheep-grazed turf

Or the special wild corner
Where bird, insect and beast
Live on a steep ravine
Where early purple orchids
And cowslips can be seen

The best stretches of countryside
Not touched by artificial fertiliser
Nor drained or improved
Where natural plant and animals hide
Is where I'd like to die.

Dora Doyle

SNOWFLAKES

Snowflakes falling, soft as a sigh
Dancing, weaving and tumbling down
Whispering gently as they float from on high
Clothing the earth in a lily-white gown.

Faster and faster the flakes start to fall
Whirling, twirling and swirling around
The wind whips them up in a miniature squall
Then dashes them frenziedly down to the ground.

A snowy white carpet has dropped from the sky
Covering the squalor, enhancing the view
The scene is revealed as the clouds scurry by
Pristine! Unsullied! Immaculate! New!

J Horsley

TOMMY

Tommy, the boy so young and so shy,
Tommy, the boy that I passed by.
His gentle eyes so wistful and sad,
Gazed into mine, but I treated him bad.
I was young also; too young to know,
Of the hearts I was breaking, 'cos they didn't show.
All I wanted was to laugh and to dance,
And flirt with the boys, so handsome and smart.
Tommy lived with his sister; an orphan was he,
Only a teenager, just like me.
The first one to bring me home from a dance,
Because he was shy, he hadn't a chance.
His hands were rough from tanning the hide,
But all his emotion was hidden inside,
And as I kept my nose in the air,
Little I knew of Tom's despair.
Each Saturday afternoon he would pace
Around the store, just to look at my face.
As I dealt with the customers' fare,
I too, would peep at him, standing there.
Then one night I collected my coat to go home,
From the Saturday dance, the Firemen's Ball.
Whilst Tommy waited at the foot of the stairs,
His eyes all dreamy and young face alight.
But I swept on by to somebody else,
And left him forlorn, whispering 'Goodnight.'
Where are you now Tommy?

Josephine Moreau

THE PREACHER

Chase the wild word -
The voice in the pulpit -
Cry in the wilderness, few came to hear -
Row upon row
Of empty chairs yawning
Bounced back each word with resonant jeer,
High flying rafters - each loud call echoes,
Ripples the dust from its ancient recluse,
Nought but the sound of the voice in the shadows,
Few come to listen - no 'absence' excuse.
Faith was the theme
Of that hard laboured message,
Gems of philosophy cunningly placed;
Wisdom - experience - harnessed together,
Words like a wild horse
Tethered and braced,
Out to the far wall - broken in flight -
Fought with the tick of the angry clock wandering
Emptiness caught in the struggling light;
Patient the handful gathered there pondering
Words rolled like waves
On a turbulent sea.
Only one there, deciphered the message,
Only the speaker -
           The speaker was me!

M Mackinnon-Pattison

MEMORIES

Sometimes you feel life passes you by.
Of course it will if you don't try!
You mustn't ever give up hope
For then you'll win and you can cope.

The worst thing of all can happen, I fear,
Losing a loved one is so hard to bear.
Good memories are so precious, I find,
A solace to heal a troubled mind.

But why rely on memories gone?
Why not create a present one!
Find something to do that's a different diversion -
Such a relief for a difficult situation.

Don't sit at home to worry and fret,
'Get up and go' is the best advice yet!
Time doesn't heal, but you can find
Being busy can help to ease your mind.

At 65, perhaps a hopeless mission?
To learn to drive was my decision.
At 67, I felt such elation
I passed my test, what celebrations!

I'm so grateful I decided to try,
Now life doesn't have to pass me by.

Ethel Hutchinson

LIFE

Life's made up of little things
That people say and do
Happiness and all it brings
Are made by me and you
What's the use of being sad?
Going along life's way
Let yourself be very glad
For each and every day
No matter just how ill you are
Just look around and view
Others worse than you by far
And many smiling too
Have a smile, a laugh and fun
You'll have so many friends
Go out to enjoy the lovely sun
Until your journey ends.

M P John

VOICES OF THE OCEAN

Oh voices of the ocean,
Voices of the sea.
Let me hear your watery voice,
Sing your song to me.

Let me hear the crashing
Sounds of waves.
Let me hear your echoes
In your seaside caves.

Oh mammals of the ocean,
Creatures of the sea.
Let me hear your gentle sounds
Sing your song to me.

Jackie Culley

SLEEPING ACCOMMODATION

It's my place, my space
They call it the black hole of Staveley
I just call it well lived in
They've named it the tip
So what it's my tip
Everything has a place
The drawers are packed with hand-me-downs
So truth be known it's not my fault
But blame lies within those
Who see me as a needy cause
Admittedly I have acquired things
I'm just like any other
To prove this point just look at yourself
And so you will discover.
My bed's a mess my mother says
Up until her weekend washday
The sheets hang loose to the floor
Reason - for ease to enter and depart
On school days with an early start.
The floor no longer can be seen
Carpeted by discarded clothes
I clear a path like shifting snow
To give direction on where to go.
But that's not all discarded here
Cups and plates with crumbs from snacks
Things I have not returned
On my journey back
To the kitchen from which they came
This is my fault I am to blame
An act of which I should be ashamed.

Jaron Hayton

The Death Of A Stallion

As a child I would wander on to the common dump
or as locals would say, playing down't lump.
The ruins of an old church could plainly be seen.
As time passed by it became grassed over like a huge village green.
We would walk to the top, you could see for miles around,
the mills and the mines on the skyline of town.
Behind the old church horses ran wild.
I gave the head stallion the great name of 'Thunder'!
When he thought the herd was in any danger, Thunder would
jump the fence and come charging forward.
The older children would get behind the stallion and drive
him up the grassy slope.
There was enough room for him to turn round at the top.
He would then rear on his hind legs showing his mighty strength
before galloping back down.
The sound from his hooves was why I gave Thunder his name.
Everyone jumped to one side as he made his escape to join the
waiting herd.
I was always so scared for my wonderful steed.
On that fateful day I went to see Thunder.
I knew something was going to go wrong.
There were more children than ever to chase my mighty stallion.
Once again he jumped the farmer's fence to protect his herd,
As he began his final climb, the children drove him much harder.
What was one childish prank, now became an act of slaughter!
Thunder had no time to turn, he just flew off the old church like
the flying 'Pegasus'.
The children scattered as he fell on to the rocks below,
leaving me to cry all alone!
The herd gathered round to look at Thunder, but turned away
when they knew the fate he was under.
It was as if to say, 'The king is dead, long live the king.'

Later that tearful day the farmer came to drag poor
Thunder away.
But I still lay flowers on his would be grave, to this
very day!
Thunder will now be running on Heaven's great plains.
He will take the lead at every stampede!
My friend the truly magnificent steed!

Ken Pendlebury

YES OR NO?

Have you finally made a decision?
Stopped yourself struggling so,
One minute you say you are coming
The next you're not going to go.
I've booked and I've cancelled your table,
But I can re-book it I know,
Please can you make a decision?
All it takes is a straight yes or no.
If you can't afford it, then don't come,
If you can, then you simply say yes,
Cos I don't really know, if you're coming or not,
I might as well just take a guess.
If it's cos you don't know what you're wearing
Stop it and make up your mind!
If you look in the wardrobe it's in there,
It's not really that hard to find.
After you've read my words of wisdom
Please will you just decide?
Just give me a definite answer,
My patience has been tested and tried.

Kazzie Ingram

LET HER SLEEP

She sleeps safely tonight
her head,
her heart resting weary feet.
Dreaming safely
quietly being asleep.

I feel her breathe
so I know she's there,
peacefully collecting the night air.
Silence fills the room
surrounding the bed on which she dreams,
I watch her for a little while
safely secure in her deep sleep.
She's warm to touch
her life being, exceeding her skin,
not a murmur
only the sound of her breathing out . . .
then in.

I will comfort her
protect her through the horrors of night,
for when the sun dawns
she will wake safely back into my life.
Gently for now,
let her sleep
safely in my arms,
never out of reach.

C Leith

MEANDERING

Moments meander from one to each next
Seconds pass politely
Lightly licking my lips
Seeking safe names
Stained by my findings
Winding my way around
Twisting and turning
Learning lessons at last
Listing likes and dislikes alike
Like little white lies applied to logic
Bleaker than black
Taking me back to motion
Moments meander from one to each next
Seconds pass politely
Tightly holding cold thought
Caught between actions.

Melvyn Hampson

THE DEPARTURE

I wandered down to the water's edge,
There was no one there but me;
I felt the wind upon my face,
It was a pleasant place to be.
I spied the tall ships in the bay
With their unfurling sails of white,
And stood and watched, and watched some more,
As they prepared to sail from sight.
With my heart aboard, I smelled the tang
Of the salt air on the day;
And gently walked without my heart,
As the tall ships sailed away.

B Colebourn

LOCKERBIE

On a dark December evening
As dusk began to fall,
Preparations for Christmas
Were being made by young and old.
Lights shone from out the windows
In that peaceful little town
When a blinding flash
A screeching noise
A plane came screaming down.
It wiped out Sherwood Crescent
On that dark cold winter's night
The fires and the carnage
Were a sickening, fearsome sight.
For some it was the shortest day
December the twenty-first
For some it was the longest day
No Christmas for them this year
With courage and quiet dignity
They went about their work
Volunteers, rescue teams
Tirelessly they searched.
Dogs scratching in the earth
Some with bleeding paws,
Not one survivor
Did they find, in their search.
Dignitaries came, the shock was great
As they stood beside the hole
Heads bowed in the sunshine
That cold December morn.
Nothing left of homes
That had once stood there
A table standing upright
In the smoke-filled air,

Tributes, condolences, flowers
Were sent from near and far
The only way that people
Could show the sorrow in their hearts
Flowers to a little girl
On the footpath by the church
Told of the friend she had made
How he felt and hurt
The only glimmer of light that shone
From that little Scottish town
Was the courage of its people
As they walked around
A boy who lost his family
Showed a brave face to the world
Father, mother, sister
In vain the rescuers searched
How can man's inhumanity
Justify this terrible deed
Bodies falling from the sky
Over the Scottish fields
American families waiting
For loved ones returning home
Realisation dawning
Knowing they would never come
December nineteen eighty-eight
Will stay in our memories
When on that dark cold winter's night
A plane fell on Lockerbie.

Doreen Moscrop

The Vision Of The Sunflower
(Dedicated to my daughter Paula who died on 18th October 1996 aged 19 years)

On waking from the depths of sleep
Wondrous images appear
Shimmering mandalas of the mind
Focusing, centring, closing clear.
A butterfly, a bee, a ram,
A fountain cascading bright,
An eagle spreads its wings to fly
From out the realms of night

This morning I stood on the petal of a sunflower
A golden path before me lie
As I looked towards its middle dark
Life's scroll unrolled before my eye.
Onward into that nucleus deep
Stumbling along each day
Man must reach the depths of man
To find the truth, the path, the way.

Amidst the dark and awesome depth
There lay some labelled seeds
I stooped to look and read each one
And God's message was revealed
Love, comfort, guidance, patience, peace,
Many more were there to find
As the shuttered lens of the camera of life
Was blinking in my mind.
I gazed in awe as I saw the Lamb
Aloft on that cross so high
To that centre of God may all men reach
Someday before they die.

I pray that every human being
Will walk that path one day
Pick up one seed and bring it back
And plant it along the way.
Nurture it and watch it grow
And it too could grow tall and strong
And it would give so many seeds
And pass the message on.

As the vision of the sunflower faded from my eyes
It had revealed life's meaning often lost
In these days of earth's demise.
I knew this morn' that the path I'd glimpsed
Led to every human heart
God's sunflower seeds are lying there
Just germinating in the dark.

Catherine Thorburn

AUTUMN STORM

Pale sun shines, and erstwhile storm clouds linger.
Some leaden, some with mirror-like reflection
Highlighting sailor-blue patches, which open, move,
And close at the touch of nature's fingers.

Yet whinberry stalks sparkle and glisten;
Saturated earth voids into river and stream.
White water where lately tranquillity presided;
Tumbling cascade demanding witnesses listen.

Swifter than thought the reborn storm rages,
Black chariot clouds race with urgent mission.
The moor disappears with awesome confusion
As Gods of the storm escape from their cages.

J Maurice Wilson

A MEASURED ARREST

I was arrested whilst writing by the Poetic Police.
  My crime? Too much rhyme.
    They said it must cease.

I was accused of simile and gross personification.
  They demanded I accompany them
    To the Poetic Police Station.

There, charges were recited in sonorous verse.
  They urged me to confess or else it be worse.

I was charged with over-rhyming without
  due care and attention and trapped in a
    cliché, I feel I should mention

that the police were stereotypical; one pleasant
  and one hard, who then orated in my
    face that in there, he was the bard!

I asked for a phone call to get Legal Aid
  they refused me this request and insisted I played
    the villain in this act.

The curtain then fell.
  The judge gave me five years, alone in this cell.

My verse found me guilty as its rhyme clearly shows.
  The judge said 'Hard labour . . . and you'll serve it in prose!'
    So now here in Walton I bide out my time
      in iambic pentameters
        though none, by law, rhyme.

H Stewart

THE SUNDAY UNCLES

They'll never detrain again
In this neck of the sturdy workout,
The two uncles from Smokechester;
Those tall, kind, gauge staunch men,
Their ale enlarged footfalls along the hall,
Their loud Millshire voices for tea:
Brothers with cancer in the familiar.

Sunday evening:
Boiled eggs and papistical church bells,
Westernised Sol in its Carnaby garish;
'The Golden Shot' unfired.
The dad upstairs,
After-pub tired.
Suddenly the Mystical city has smells!

Sit sinking on the sofa,
Bathyscape deepening
The cushions and springs,
The doublet of suited colossals,
Late afternoon's best things.
Those gentle Titans

In their nicotine oriflambed
Off-straight ties;
Their half open
Half closed flies.
F with a sand curried watch
He captured in Tunisia.

They're dead now, always dead,
Eyes awake to their completed cancer.
The sofa's shape soon reasserted
And I am none the wiser.

Charles Butler

SHEVINGTON

The idyllic scene of that lovely house
Is etched upon my mind
Built on an incline close to woods
It really was divine
Having lived in the country
And yet being close to town
Was having the best of both worlds
With none of the sounds
The name of the house was Brookside
Opposite a babbling brook
The woods a few yards away
Was simply a magic nook
We stayed there just four years
A market gardener bought the place
We go there to visit friends
And find it hasn't lost its grace.

M Tickle

WHY?

Why has the elephant got such a great big nose?
I thought my own substantial, but it's small compared to those!
Mine does all I ask of it (and sometimes a bit more!)
But having a trunk must be absolutely deafening when you snore!

Why do older ladies dye their hair lilac or blue?
I mean, it's hardly natural - it wouldn't fool me or you!
Are we really supposed to look at them admiringly and think,
'She looks so young! What lovely hair! If only mine were pink!'

Why do we say 'Get off that wall! You'll have an accident, you see;
And if you fall and break your legs, don't come running to me!'
There's lots of curious questions, but the one that baffles me, is
'Why have I only got two legs, when the Isle of Man has three?'

J Grayson

A SUMMER'S DAY

Clear blue summer skies
cotton wool clouds on high.
Golden sands, warm underfoot
with the stream rippling by.

Rock pools cold and green
in them tiny creatures hide.
Upon the silver-grey rocks
seaweed, mussels, limpets cling.

Children's buckets and spades
lie forgotten upon the sand.
As they cavort amongst the waves
oblivious to worldly things.

Sand dunes rise above the beach
a world of gorse and heather.
Where rabbits and skylarks roam
away from human reach.

Children's laughter, then a silent pause
as overhead the helicopter drones.
Then back to play amongst the waves
not a thought as to the cause.

A dark cloud appears. A worried parent.
'Have you seen, only little, wandered off.'
'Wouldn't go far, I'm sure.' Frightened now.
'The water, she cannot swim, loves the water.'

Suddenly the sun appears. 'She's here.'
'Playing in the rock pools, catching crabs.'
'Knew she wouldn't go far. What a relief.'
It's a lovely summer's day again. No fear.

Lydia E Stanton

JOHN LENNON

If John Lennon was alive today
       Imagine if you can
If John Lennon was alive today.
       Dream if you wish.
If John Lennon was alive today
       To write to strive, in his way.
Give us thoughts, a musical bliss
       For the world, a Lennon kiss.
His writing's great, in any form
His own pen, or with Paul to bond.
Would he write of a dictator cold
Using cowardice, fascism,
           We've seen of old.
People cleansed, from their homes
Their only crime, not good enough.
Would Lennon fight for their right
To live with democracy, in every sight?
If John Lennon was alive today.

Harry Livesey

CHEERING FLAMES

For many people who are growing old,
Who live with relatives in modern homes,
For those in council flats or nursing care,
One comfort is denied when winds blow cold.

Once, as days grew dark with rain or snow,
Their homes were warmed by flickering, living flames
They drew their chairs beside the cheering warmth.
Happy and content to see the firelight's glow.

A fire is like a friend who cares for you.
It 'talks' in cheerful noises, crackles, bubbles.
Its flames show shifting pictures, wreathed in smoke.
When it dies, the spirit dies a little too.

It matters not how bright and warm and clean
A modern room and heating is to the young.
Warmth everywhere, without the work to do.
Still most old folk would choose the fire's gleam.

Enid Broe

BREEZES

Gentle leaves embrace the air swirling them to the ground,
Dancing along with the wind in a waltz of love.
Rain cleanses anything it may have found,
Taking care as leaves rise up above.
Falling into the river, trapped in her torrid flow,
Sail on beautiful water run with the current, off you go.

Bowing to the clouds the trees now pay homage,
As wind blows their branches almost inside out.
Destroying and dropping golden coloured foliage,
Like galleons riding a stormy sea of doubt.
A carpet of abundant colours skate and cover the floor.
Gentle breezes blow away cobwebs hanging around life's door.

Wind kissing gently on the river, a welcome sight to see.
I hear you trickling and calling in the night,
Rippling, running faster, beckoning me,
Such a welcoming and inviting sight.
Swirling, bashing against small rocks and stones.
When your journey's ended, in the oceans you will be home.

Denise Threlfall

MOTHER

There's one thing that we never do, oh darling Mother mine,
We don't realise it's God's sweet love that make your dear eyes shine.
We don't realise the struggle that you had, when you were young,
The worry and the heartache, the sacrifice unsung,
We don't realise the sorrow and the wrinkles caused with care,
Or how lonely you feel Mother, when you see Dad's vacant chair.
We never realise Mother, how you always *played the game,*
Or ever stop to think how sweet and precious is your name,
We don't realise your growing old, until your hair turns grey,
Or how weary you feel sometimes, at the closing of the day,
We'll never realise Mother, how much you will be missed,
Until the day, for the last time, those dear, sweet lips we've kissed.

Eric McBride

ODE TO MY VW BEETLE

I'll defend you
honour you
dote on you
get personal with you
I love you

You poison the air
and little children's lungs
you send me to near death
regularly
you bring out the adventurer in me
I love you

Yes
I'm certain this is love
and . . . y' know
in a strange Beetle sort of way
I think you love me too.

J Gordon

MONARCH OF THE NIGHT

There shines the moon in all its silver glory,
Piercing the silken smooth darkness of the night,
Its radiant spell cast all around,
And dappled patterns lie upon the land
Where moonbeams penetrate the leafy trees
Turning this woodland glade into magic ground.

Muted whisperings among the grass beneath the trees,
Cautious rustlings where dead leaves have drifted
Awakened are the creatures of the night;
Large or small they venture forth with care
And blend with the dancing moon-shadows
Like some elusive, teasing, woodland sprite.

And up above, high in the ancient oak,
Unmoving, all seeing, statuesque in his dignity
There sits that noble fowl;
For surely of all the creatures of the night
He must be the rightful king -
His Majesty - the owl!

Imperious lord of all he surveys,
As silently he sits and stares,
Well conscious of his power,
For who would dare to flaunt his reign
Or question his royal right to rule
As he broods in his oaken tower.

For whether at rest on his treetop throne
Or silently riding the midnight air
In ghostly, swooping flight,
Salute to you, most beautiful bird,
With power and wisdom so well endowed,
The Monarch of the night!

Bernard Laughton

SUNDAY SCHOOL ANNIVERSARIES

We walked a mile to Sunday school
Every Sunday morning.
'Now mind you behave yourselves today'
Was the constant warning.

The chapel, it was called Waterside,
For the river flowed closely by.
It was almost bursting at the side
When anniversary time was nigh.

The anniversary came once a year:
We really thought this was swell.
For this was when we got a new dress
And hat and shoes as well.

I sat on the platform with the rest,
And timidly said my piece.
We were all quite nervous -
But afterwards we had such a feast.

We sailed on a barge down the river -
This really was a great treat.
The organ was softly playing
And a shop was there to buy sweets.

We returned from the trip to a service
To thank God for a wonderful day.
We each got some sweets and a sixpence:
It seemed like a fortune, those days

When we look back to childhood days,
The highlights of our lives
Were the very simple pleasures
On which we all did thrive.

Iris Covell

MILLENNIUM COUNTDOWN

The Almighty looked down on the earth one day
And thought what a terrible mess.
One half of the population were mad
And the others were all under stress.
The trees and the fields didn't look quite as green
As he had first meant them to be.
The beaches polluted, the air was all foul
And look at the state of the sea.
The people were wrecking this place he had made
With their pollution and wars and their fire.
It looked as though all was now lost for the world
But still the Almighty's a tryer.
Perhaps he could sort it, make everything right
He'd do something drastic, he'd give them a fright.
He started with heat that was hot beyond reason
Then ice, snow and rain that was out of its season.
An earthquake or two and then some raging seas
The horrors went on, man was brought to his knees.
But still they learnt nothing man sings his own tune
While still waging war they cast eyes to the moon.
No said the Almighty, I'll not have this race
You seek yet to ruin another fine place.
The earth is a mess and man has to see
This planet was given a blessing from me.
To be nurtured and cared for and kept free from pain
The Almighty was sad, he had laboured in vain.
The people were frightened some started to cry
Where else could they go, and they looked to the sky.
The Almighty looked down he had scared them for sure
He'd take a big chance and give them a year more.
So has anything changed, not one thing I fear
The world's still a mess, the millennium draws near.

Lynne Marie White

SOMEONE

Someone to love you
        someone who cares,
A heart filled with love
        that was my Clair's.

A smile in the morning
        my light in the night,
Eyes filled with love
        made everything right,

There is at present no tomorrow
        for we had yesterday,
Just waiting for the moment
        that is our today.

We lived with so much happiness
        then there was so much more,
With kissing as a way of life
        was what our lips were for.

There is never one moment
        she is not in my mind,
Now there is just a dent in her pillow
        it's all I can find.

Dark shadows on the ceiling
        no pictures on the wall,
A mind full of memories
        as I wait for her call.

Grey skies on a sunny morning
        and a heart running on cold,
Rainbows that are hidden
        there will be more I am told.

Stars that are twinkling
        but now not for me,
Just yesterday's comet passing
        is all that I see.

Jimmy

THE HOPE INSIDE

The hope inside
Slowly died.

The stolen dreams
Faded before my eyes;
Turned to nightmares
Vaporised.

It's raining pain
I'm drowning in hurt.
It became an aimless existence
When you killed the hope inside.

The song is finished
The dance is over now.
The meteoric rise has ended.
But the pieces are broken
It all just fell apart
I've searched the lowlands and the highlands
But there's no mend for the broken heart.

We're all babbling in foreign tongues
It's still unclear where it all went wrong.
I pleaded with you, I broke down, I cried,
But you still killed the hope inside.

Maxx Maynard

The Social Revolution

Life sails repetitiously
Upon swift flowing tides
Moving faster with the possession of years
Societies left stranded
In a technological dream
In a revolution that supplies its own fears

Change exploded upon people
Without warning or guilt
Disturbing the foundations they thought were secure
Change structured uncertainty within everyone's brain
Creating the roads they're expected to explore

Yesterday was predictable
Protective and calm
Meandering sedately through the slow country lanes
Yesterday was possessive
With an intimate charm
Providing security with its limited gains

Tomorrow teases the present
Persecutes the obsessed
Whose ideas are continually out of date
Many dreams are invited to construct their belief
In a cold material paradise tampering with fate

Money is the spirit
The clock is the soul
Of this stress-filled environment possessed by time
The escalation is terminal
Every human is drawn
To the social revolution forever altering the mind.

David Bridgewater

ANSAFONE PHOBIA

Talking on the telephone
Is fine - but it's absurd
If I ever get the ansafone
I cannot say a word.

Talking to a friend
I can talk for weeks and weeks
But my monologue will end
When I hear those dreaded beeps.

I start to go quite red
And my face goes hot and cold
And the words I wanted said
Are forever left untold.

I get into a fluster
Though my message I prepare
And all my courage muster
But the willpower isn't there.

Like a stranded fish I splutter
And my thoughts all drift away
And my heart it starts to flutter
And I'm lost for things to say.

But chatting on the telephone
Is fun, I must admit
As long as there's no ansafone
To cause a frightful fit!

Chérianne Wren

SADNESS

Why do I feel so sad these days
Why do I feel so bad always
My friends are there but the line is busy
They cannot be got and I'm in a tizzy
I feel so alone now Reg has gone
He really hasn't been away very long
He was my true love and my life
Reg loved me dearly as a friend and wife
No one to talk to and ask questions of
No one to care for me now, he's with God
Our lives together were really great
He was so special, he was my best mate
Twenty beautiful years we spent together
We often sailed through stormy weather
I loved him then and I love him now
I'm trying to live again somehow
I was lucky to have close friends
But when I'm desperate they're never in
I feel so much pain and it won't go away
I feel like I'm dying inside today
I hurt everywhere, I have physical pain
Which doesn't help at the end of the day
I'm trying so hard to pull myself up
And be thankful for the Lord above
I passed an exam the first in my life
But no friend was home and I was in such strife
I try to find someone at home
Just when I'd given up and felt so alone
At home I found a very dear friend
To tell about my exam in the end
I would like to get closer to God today
I hope he can hear what I have to say

I want to live in this beautiful world
But I can't seem to lift this awful cloud
My Reg has gone and I must go on
Without my friends it can't be done
They have their friends and family around
Their lives are very, very sound
God forgive me for feeling this way
It's my Reg I miss at the end of the day.

Maggie Coleby

WWW//Computerspeak

WWW//computerspeak./conversations
with many people: far away from here/
modern technology//wonderful invention
isn't it?/modem, mouse and much more:
try to keep pace with the millennium/
and the dawn of a new revolution.//
html.com.browse as you please:
so many things to explore/and enjoy
never leaving the house/ no fresh air//
a social circle./written in text format
and sent down the wires.wonderful
invention isn't it?// so much to see
and do@home: all alone
thousands of people talking: never
meeting/never leaving their homes.
Is it a good thing//never writing
a letter./or hearing a human voice
on the other end of the line?
www//computerspeak./manipulation.

Nikky Braithwaite

SONS AND MOTHERS

He never left,
Just moved away,
He needed space to find himself.
A branch not severed,
But reaching out towards the light
And teased away by life's rich treasures.
Not lost,
His roots secure in love that never wavers
And in wisdom born from wrongly chaining slaves.
I watch and wait,
For in the letting go, we both find freedom
To go our separate ways, to grow
Unhindered by a sense of guilt or bound by duty.
The door is always open to come and go,
Not mine to own,
A son, a soul to love and cherish.
He will return,
He has returned,
He never really left,
Great teacher life our bond has strengthened.

Frances Allen

AFTER TIME SPENT TOGETHER

Lips of the finest wine
the briefest taste
body afire
mind in eruption.

To touch your hand
a passing caress
electric passion
lightning arcs.

In your presence
all atingle
great joy
in exhilaration.

Love reaffirmed
heart rejoicing
only statement of validity -
'I love you'.

R Colville

SONG OF THE WHALE

Sonar booms in the dark blue sea
I hear the Beluga calling me
through the tempest storm and gale
I hear the haunting song of the whale

Large Grey Humpback blowing free
diving and rising in the surging sea
from Arctic wastes and sunset pale
I hear the haunting song of the whale

Lord and master of the deep
the portals of Neptune's kingdom keep
thrashing asunder from head to tail
I hear the haunting song of the whale

Entombed in oceans wide and deep
by man his filthy lucre reap
as hunters seek their Holy Grail
I hear no more the song of the whale.

James Adams

BARFLY

She sits alone by
the bar.
Eyes pink from many
nights before.
Bloated.
A monster of her former
shadow.

Lost in the
smoke
of a thousandth
cigarette.
Thoughts of drunken
sexual encounters,
seeking
companionship.

Finding it only in
the next drink.

Michele Conroy

POORLY BABS

My daughter's in a turmoil,
she's not too well I fear.
Not only is her iron low,
she's completely out of gear.

A thyroid or a prolapse
are only but a few.
She's tired nearly all the time,
me thinks the change is due.

But as she is a person,
to really up and go,
She's keeping up her dancing
tho' maybe rather slow.

So time that she was sorted,
and put back on the track,
Then she can get on with her life
and give us all some flack.

M Goodier

REFLECTIONS

I remember sitting on the pram
Ration coupons, bread and jam
Sunday mornings - half an egg
Lisle stockings on my legs
Gas mask on my face, to try
Stop something nasty from the sky
The store horse falling in the snow
Landing thick and white years ago
Warm sunny days, babbling brooks
Frog spawn and jars of newts
Walking barefoot, toes covered in tar
Only in summer and not too far
Pockets stuffed with apples and pears
Taken from orchards without a care
Darting shadows on the walls which seemed to grow
While toasting bread from the fire's glow
Tastes, smells and memories of days gone by
Haunt me still - I don't know why.

D Brooks

COLD

The icy world in Antarctica
So dull, so lonely and cold
The freezing waves like whales' jaws
Roaring, roaring, roaring

The cold wintry snow storms
Covering everything in its path
And the ice looked so clear,
So cold and so hard
When you try to touch the ice and snow
It sends a shiver up your spine
It's so cold, so cold, so cold

If you fall in the icy sea or rivers
You will shout out in pain
Like daggers that have been put in your body
And have been pulled away one by one
The water, rivers, wind and rain
Are so icy so chilly and raw and cold

Samantha Neithercut (10)

EVENING SHADOWS

The trees are gauntly black, against a leaden sky
the rain has stopped - leaving millions of tiny dewdrops
                                    on the branches high
so pretty in the fading light, sparkling like diamonds in the twilight

Now the sky has changed to a deep blue and gold
enhancing this picture to behold
a breeze ruffles the trees - and now the diamonds have gone
                                    into the pending night

Evening shadows are falling fast
and the sky is again grey cast
but between the dark clouds a touch of pink appears now
as though the lovely colours want to stay somehow,
before the night descends and this lovely picture ends
and so . . . the day thou gavest Lord is ending
the darkness falls at thy behest.

Edna Parrington

MOTHER NATURE'S CHILD

O, she passes now with footstep light
Her fragrant airs a'blowing
o'er hill and dale and woody glen
To the farmer in the fields a'sowing

Carried on a gentle breeze
By lake and rippling stream
Through green and verdant meadowland
To purple mountains' rugged seam

The goodness of the land is hers
To the birds she too is known
The sweetened breaths of morning air
These she all doth own

When evening falls and dark shades too
And secret voices murmur
And plaintive call sounds off so clear
Then they talk of her

Mistress of the waving corn
Spirit of the wild
Voice of chill, mysterious night
Is Mother Nature's Child.

N A Corker

SWEET ROSEBUD OF DELIGHT

I sing for you a love song
Soft as an angel's kiss.
To send you calmly sailing
Enchanted seas of bliss.
Within your mother's arms now
Sweet rosebud of delight:
Into sleep to rock you,
So safe and warm this night.

Come daddy's little darling:
Close now those pretty eyes,
That send us into raptures
As love wears no disguise:
I sing for you a love song,
A gentle melody.
Telling of the happiness
You bring so joyfully.

I sing for you a love song,
A lilting lullaby:
Soft as snow-white thistledown
On summer's fragrant sigh.
So in your cosy cradle,
As moon and stars shine bright:
You'll drift to peaceful dreamland,
Till morning's welcome light.

Violet M Corlett

DAWN TO DUSK

Daylight breaks on a lonely sky
as night shadows slip away.
We earthly mortals might wonder why
this mystery day after day
we take for granted these wonderful things
for which we have nothing to pay.
Something new each new day brings,
and goes on day after day.
While we sleep miracles unfold.
How they are done, who can say?
We believe what we are told,
repeated day after day,
as we fold back the morning curtain
on a world bright and gay.
We can never be more certain
that night will follow day.

William Banks

DREAMS

During the long hours of the night,
Our dreams in their entirety,
Seem so real, so lifelike, so . . . there.
And yet,
When we wake to the light of the early morning sun,
Our dreams are forgotten,
Stored deep in our memories, our thoughts, our past,
As thought they never were.

Kathryn Millington

THE COUNCIL DELEGATION

The Council delegation,
Eighteen people smartly dressed,
Standing in the street.
Outside number two three eight
They are standing in the rain.

It's not only the weather
Whipping up a storm.
But this is no storm in a teacup.
The whole of the terrace is labelled.
The label reads 'unsafe'.

The terrace marked for demolition:
It's the end of life down here.
It's the end of our community,
Not just the terrace walls,
And no one seems to care.

The Council delegation
Their cars parked all down the street.
They take up both the sides,
Blocking all the access,
And ignoring all the protests.

The traffic starts to meet.
There's a hearse caught in the mayhem,
With a bus and a courier's van,
A milk float trundles through the fuss.
And the people keep looking on.

The Council delegation
Have aired their words to us.
The dead have trundled off from view
And the living all live one.
And no one gives a toss.

Kathryn J Hayward

UNTITLED

The girl with the gun strolled into the room,
Her mission to send her foe to the tomb;
She was stunningly dressed in flashy cord shorts
And tee shirt of colours of eye catching sorts;
And no one could know that her presence was doom.

All that was required was one shot from the gun
To make sure her mission was perfectly done;
The girl with the gun then strolled from that place
And vanished for all time leaving no trace;
Of feelings of guilt and remorse she had none.

Her victim was lying spread out on the floor:
Through flesh of her body the hot bullet tore;
Her life from her poured with each painful breath;
Her cheeks turned to white with the pallor of death
As she lay in pools which filled with her gore.

Nigel Miller

SPRING

The tulips the daffodils are all out in bloom
Oh what a joy to see them in your room
To know life is bursting awakening once more
After the cold lonely winter the flowers you adore
The buds on the trees the blossoms in array
You know that spring is here and summer's on the way
Nature has awoken from its long cold sleep
No more snow, fog and ice and most of all sleet
The dear Planet Sun, oh where have you been
It seems so long ago since we felt your last beam
So we will enjoy the wonders of life
Even getting up each day will be very nice.

Patricia Davis

THE LITTLE GREY CHURCH

There's a lantern outside the little grey church,
it shines with a pale mellow glow.
The berries and holly are trimming the porch
and the gravestones are hidden in snow.
The bells aren't yet ringing, it isn't quite dawn,
the stars in the sky are still bright.
You can see Jack Frost's footprints crossing the lawn
and the patterns he made in the night.
Before very long the children will stir, and the
villagers' clocks will chime,
And the cattle will low from the fields and the byres,
The news that it's Christmastime.
The music will sound from the little grey church,
sending a note of good cheer,
The people will sing and the carols will ring;
'Merry Christmas and a Happy New Year.'

I Moor

AN ORPHAN

A thrush was hopping, on the lawn,
looking for a snack.
When, he went and came upon,
a worm, upon its back.
He grabbed it quick and ate it up,
which made me really mad.
Cause he'd gone and went and gobbled up,
my dear old slimy dad.
Oh my gosh, not again!
He went and grabbed another.
I think that I'm an orphan now,
cause he went and ate me mother!

B Boertien

THE STORMS OF LIFE

Every plant and flower in my garden had died
The storm ripped up every tree
Every living thing
had been tossed to and fro
by the winds
the very landscape had changed
The colour of the day
was suddenly different

Everything I had invested
prayer and care in
was gone
destroyed and forgotten
so quickly

Looters came and stole
what the storm had spared
and I wept so deep inside
clutching my baby
'At least we are alive.'

All those plans and dreams
just dust and broken artefacts
and to my surprise
the sun came jump
and it was blue skies
'Now you are alive.'

Stephen Starkie

A Musical Journey

An old man sits with a gentle smile
His long grey hair under a hat
Singing softly accompanied by a guitar
Songs of the past seem to fill the air
The sound of his voice
With a sad lament
Seems to create echoes
Of distant memories

A swish of the drums and
The tap of a foot
Quickly changes the beat
Bringing laughter and joy
The man on the accordion
Squeezes the music with all his strength
The old man no longer looks sad
There are smiles once again

A lady stands silently but not alone
Reaching out in the darkness
She can no longer see
But the music calms her
Knowing someone is still there
The applause is deafening.
The strains of the music fade.

Betsey Prose

To My Husband - On Our Golden Wedding Day

It's 50 years ago today since I became your wife,
Although we've had our ups and downs, we've had a happy life.
My love won the Derby on that Saturday afternoon,
The day that we got married, on the 5th of June.

For better and for worse we told each other on that day,
And with love and trust, together we have come a long, long way.
So now there's only just one thing that I must surely do,
And tell you, my dear husband, I'm glad I married you.

E Kay

MY WINDOW

I look out my window, what do I see
The magnificent bridge peering at me.
I look out my window - look down our road
Land full of poppies' stories somewhere for young or old.
St Patrick's Church once stood.
I like to think the poppies are saying, while swaying,
'People all stay good. People all give love.

Take a walk down our road - Spike Island
Catalst Museum right.
So many visitors both day and night.
Walking on further you end near the town,
Queen's Hall, look, staged here are many famous shows.
Which year after year come and go.

Old Town Hall, a waterfall
Grand library, art college down hall.
St Paul's church, seating all round.
Wonderful place pausing with thoughts both feet on the ground.

Halton, Widnes, we don't make a fuss
From here take a bus.
Morrison's, our new market hall
T J Hughes, many shops, we have it all.
See for yourself, take a trip, have a ball.

G Rowen

IN THE EYES OF THE GODS

Look up Dear Lord up into the clouds send the Spirit
That is drifting slowly by and by
Powerful minds and glowing figures
A multitude of events pass before my eyes.
The big silver cross that hangs in the church
Sculptures that are on the shelf
The lovely mosaic on the ceiling
The speed of light is shining
And in comes this wonderful feeling.
The organ that is playing in the background
And the hymns that are ready to be sung
The congregation that gathers in time
Happiness in the community
And to enjoy another year is fine.
Look up into the sky and dream of the Spirit
Beautiful white clouds that send us peace and joy with it
The best years are to be cherished
A star is falling from the sky
The moon is still glowing
And the words that I say are flowing.
Whistling wind that is blowing strong
Feeling free the days are long.
I dream of the creation the sun and the stars
The black night that's upon us
That is certain to go far.
Look up in the clouds
As far as the eye can see
A glowing picture of the future
And the days in life are free.

C Kirkham

GETTING RID

I've cleaned the mirror
With a skilful swipe.
And scrubbed the bath
Till it's gleaming white.
I've polished the table
To a glossy glow.
I won't slow down
I'm on a roll.
I've cleaned the windows
Till they're shiny bright.
And the furniture
Above head height.
The door jam's been done
And so has the loo.
Won't stop till I'm done
Not even for a brew.
I've vacuumed every corner
The curtains and rug.
I'm sure I've got rid of
This millennium bug.

Helusia Shire

LANCASHIRE MOORS

See the beauty of the wild moors
With freedom to roam, no closed doors.
Nature at her finest, different shades of green.
Wildlife abundant on the ground, in trees.
People you meet bid the time of day,
A nod, smile as they pass your way.
God in his glory on the wild moors
Freedom to roam with no closed doors.

J Morris

MIRACLES

'I don't believe in miracles!'
I heard that a cynic said.
For those all around him
must have passed over his head.
Who, seeing a seed grow,
to become a flower or a tree,
could help but think it a miracle,
there for all to see.

Then again, a baby,
born all new and fresh.
A miracle created
from your very own flesh!
How then does a pigeon
freed miles away from a basket,
know the way to its home loft?
I wish that I could ask it!

The same can be asked
of those migrating birds.
Animals travelling
in flocks and herds.
They go for days
without map or compass.
Ask humans to do that -
then hear the rumpus!

But the greatest of miracles
I've known in my life,
was the day my beloved one,
became my wife!

Brain Humphreys

A NOSTALGIC FAREWELL

Goodbye old school, you served your purpose well
and all who studied 'neath your roof could tell
of dedicated teachers of the past.
Striving to teach us things that they hoped would last.

When I started school, those many years ago,
I had no smart new uniform to show,
just a little pinafore covering my togs,
a hankie on a safety pin and a little pair of clogs.

But we were well and truly taught by teachers firm and just.
The three Rs to be mastered, good behaviour was a must.
No sport at all for girls like me, in the long ago,
instead we had to learn to knit, to darn a sock and sew.

The boys could all play football, we had a worthy team.
To win a trophy for the school was every young lad's dream.
They used to proudly take the field in stripes of black and white
We used to cheer them on their way on competition night.

Since its beginning our old school saw life in all its stages.
The aftermath of two world wars are written in its pages.
But time moves on relentlessly, and changes must be faced
and buildings just like people some day must be replaced.

So it's goodbye to the old school and welcome to the new,
with special thanks for everyone who made it all come true.
May all within its walls succeed in everything they do
and the spirit of the old school be present in the new.

Florence Pilkington

Age?

Age is a state of mind they say
And this is very true
Because your youth has been and gone
It's not the end of you
These years are meant to do the things
You longed to do before
But pressed for time
You had to wait
Until the days were yours
So now you've earned the right to choose
What you do each day
It doesn't matter about age
Or what some people say
The time is yours alone
So do the best you can
Don't be a lonely stay-at-home
Enjoy your full life's span
Believe you are just starting out
On some great holiday
But never, never, think you're old
You'll give the game away.

C Allison

Millennium 2000

Millennium 2000 is getting closer every day,
Plans made, action is now the order of the day.
Millennium Dome in Greenwich, nearly complete in every way.
What a masterpiece to behold as people weave in and out,
and tell of great wonders they have seen.

High above the city of Newcastle
the Angel Of The North stands tall and proud.
Arms outstretched as if to say,
'Let's get this millennium on its way.'

There is talk about the millennium bug,
I just don't know what it means!
Just heard it may destroy all kinds of things,
and leave us in a turmoil.

In our town of proud Preston
I'm sure glasses will be raised on high.
Everyone will sing, 'God Save Our Queen,'
on 2000 millennium day.

Kathleen Gosling

THE COAST

The Groynes stand battered by advancing waves
Like sentinels to check the shifting sands,
The rusty screws and bands bind staves
Of wood put there long since by numerous hands,
The seaweed lies atop so many boards
So green in texture and so colourful,
Attracting sea and other birds in hoards
The brown of screws, the green of weed, not dull
As are the rusting bands, some broken just like swords,
The Groynes reject the forces of Atlantic gales
They haven't moved - each board on top of board
Retained in place by iron hoops with screws, not nails,
They've stood the test of time but need repairing,
I hope the renovations and the work that's done
Is sound in budget, skill, which means no paring,
So when completed and the battle won,
The sand will stay in place, and Groynes stand proud declaring
'Sea, try and crush us with your might - your waves ton after ton,'
The sun will set time and again - we'll show no signs of wearing.

G Isherwood

MARANATHA

I am the beggar on the street,
Sitting with drooping head.
In your mercy Father,
Give me my daily bread.

I am the victim of the cheat,
The violent and the thief.
Selfishness and greed increase,
What will bring relief.

I am the child who is abused,
Neglected and in pain.
Wanting the hurt to go away
So I can laugh again.

I am the Third World worker
Toiling at a loom.
My only meal a bowl of rice,
My home a dark, bare room.

I am the tortured prisoner
In a land that is not free.
Where human rights are all denied,
Who will cry for me.

I am the voice of conscience
That never can be still.
The accuser of a world gone wrong
And filled with moral ill.

I am He that loves the world,
Who died, who suffered pain,
And who will bring God's justice
When he comes again.

D H Taylor

VENTED ANGUISH

Do not betray my trust, or I shall surely vent my anguish upon thee!
I will belittle your maligned spirit with my harsh words of vex.
Remember what you have done, as long as there is a sun,
      My anger has not yet even begun!
Betray my trust and see how evil I can be.
See the true reason why people respect me.
My words of truth will leave nothing but a bitter taste in your mouth.
How dare you betray the trust that I have bestowed upon thee!
      Now my anger has begun!
I will rain upon thee like a torrent of tears from a lonesome
                      man's heart!
I will destroy your heart and spirit, making you void of compassion
                 and feeling forever more!
These are just a couple of reasons why my anger shouldn't be vented
                      upon thee.

David Lamb

THE MIRROR IMAGE

I look into the mirror with bleary eyes
And see a reflection not telling me lies
I used to be young, lithe and strong
But now my self-image says that I'm wrong
I squeeze a pimple I can see on my face
I'm getting past it now, I'm a disgrace
I liked to look at my smiling toothpaste-smile pose
But now I'm toothless with hairs protruding from my nose.
Like the queen in 'Mirror, mirror on the wall
Tell us who is the fairest of them all'?
Just look at that ego look in my eye
I'm full of conceit like the God Narcissi
Just think about good times on looking back
Now blemishes and wrinkles enough to make the mirror crack.

Francis Arthur Rawlinson

A Realisation

I've lived my life to middle age,
through honest toil I've earned a wage.
Yet oft' in newsprint now I see,
the names of friends who have ceased to be.
From schooldays some with whom I played,
working colleagues who should have stayed
and lived their lives, have come and gone,
while fate decrees I linger on.
Making long term plans to retire,
never contemplating I would expire.

Suddenly I have changed my view,
I could be next in that fatal queue.
As my demise approaches fast,
I will live each day as though my last.
Each hour effervescing to the brim,
a happy, carefree, lucky Jim.
Eat, drink, love, laugh and cry,
hedonistic pleasure until I die.
Think kind thoughts and do good deeds
before I'm pushing up those weeds.

The miraculous conception that is man,
has a tortuous short lifetime span.
Seize the chance - enjoy each day,
you will never again pass this way.
Read these lines and know my plight,
against time no mortal man can fight;
A certainty - time marches on,
the day will dawn when you are gone.
The wonders of life are so sublime,
waste not one moment of precious time.

Harry Ashworth

IF WALLS COULD TALK

Days and weeks come and go
and so with it do the seasons.
Yet in a cottage sits an old lady
time for her, just for a moment stands still,
as she sits and thinks and reasons.

It is so peaceful in her living room
apart from the clock with its comforting tick, on the wall.
Time has stood still giving her time to recall
the happy times, the sad times, she remembers them all.

She remembers her childhood when she was small.
The smell of baking drifting through the hall
to welcome visitors who would call
as they were passing.
Was it really that long ago?

She suddenly starts to tire,
her eyelids growing heavy.
She shuts her eyes . . .
The clock on the wall keeps on ticking.
The four walls in their silence break up the gloom
with reflections of red from the fire.

No one will ever know of her loneliness
in that cosy living room
where she had once been so happy.

Hilary Turner

THE GREAT OCEANS AND SEAS

Many things have been written about the oceans and seas.
Where man dares to dive below, or skim over, on skis.
To be out in the elements, and look over wide open space,
and see the edges of the waves, like huge ruffles of lace.
It's an amazing adventure there out on the deep.
Does anything, or anyone, find time to sleep?

The excitement of the rollers are for the young and the strong,
and deep down below them are millions of fishes that throng.
They're there in another world of beautiful colours and sizes,
and when man swims amongst them, he sees lots of surprises.
He marvels at the masses, and the corals, and the life,
as each of the species survives its own kind of strife.

When their waters are calm, and not a white horse in sight,
it's especially inviting, as is a starry sky at night.
Imagine, out on the sea of blue, in a super sailing yacht,
when the land you are leaving, becomes an untouchable spot.
Then you're at the mercies of the great sea and the ocean,
where the vastness is scary, but a thrilling, memorable emotion.

The liners, the cargo ships, the fishermen and sailors,
submarines and cruisers, and the lonely lives of the whalers.
They all know the might of the great oceans and seas,
the gales, and the storms, the hot sunshine, and the breeze.
The hard days, the sleepy days, days of elation,
then stepping back on land again, to a different sensation.

Yes lots of things are associated with the great oceans and seas.
Land was discovered via them, some are warm, and some freeze.
For these oceans and seas, God made the world round,
and only land separates them, their different names to sound.
They are the waterways of the world for us men to travel
and both over and under them, their wonders still unravel.

Pauline Mole

QUEST FOR LOVE

The powerful attraction to life in a city,
for some, can bring joy, for others it's gritty.
If you stay where you are, you may think you're doomed,
to people, and life, you think you're not tuned.
So, off you go with your future at stake,
your soul to revive, and your heart to awake.
You step on the train, with your head held high,
to seek out the one thing, that money can't buy.
The anonymity of life in a city,
unknown faces, some ugly, some pretty.
The days, the months and the years go by
so do the people, in whose arms you did lie.
After all that soul searching,
you've not much to show.
A stone that was rolling,
where moss could not grow.
So, you think to yourself, where else can I go?
You travel to Paris, Vienna and Rome,
then comes a strong calling, of thoughts near to home.
Yes, maybe back home is where my destiny lies,
it's only a small town, unlike a city in size.
With your heart unawakened,
and your soul unrevived,
you step from the train,
all your hopes they have died.
At the bottom of your suitcase, though carefully packed,
lie two souvenirs, not fully intact.
There are fragments and pieces of various parts
from a box of shattered dreams,
and, a parade of broken hearts.

Martin Howard

THE DAILY RACE

Life is a daily race that everyone has to run
From birth - and unto death - yet no one here can shun

Some folks live in the fast lane - others - at a much slower pace
Some see all of life's beauty - others show a real dull face

Some climb up the 'high peaks' - in order to reach their goal
Can't they see by standing still - it's no good for their soul

All nation's people vary - their tasks in life they differ
Some - make a fortune in a day - for others - it is much stiffer

Travelling life's way for some folks - their roads are paved with gold
Others - they weave a tangled web - and from youth -
                                        they soon grow old

So, take this journey slowly - creeping - before you walk
And as you run 'the race of life'
Think clearly - before you talk.

Edna Cattermole

PROCRASTINATION

A thief broke and entered my day
Stealing my time and laying aside my plans;
Good intentions that I had mapped out
And schedules I had plotted with careful precision.
Against my will I yielded to temptation
Giving in to this devil who had sought me out,
Weakening to his persuasive desires
To lose precious time forever.

A Richard

DYSLEXIA

My friends would not acknowledge it.
My family practised laudable restraint.
My teachers despaired of me.
I despised my aberrant taint.

My tormentors did not understand.
Acknowledgement of feeling caused pain,
Cruelly subverted defences I had planned and
Plotted to anaesthetise my watchful brain.

Then you came along.
You discovered the aberrance had a name -
I was dyslexic
My inability to read was no shame.

My mists started to dissipate
The pain and hurt began to fade
But the memories and gratitude burned on
I had finally made the grade.

And now the flesh of you is gone.
The memory of you buried underneath the years
But now it rises, as bright as the dawn
And I remember you, your strength and tears.

You told me I could do anything and I tried.
They said I couldn't make it.
They lied.

Caroline Elizabeth Ashton

MY BRADDER WOOD

A wooded mile on the side of a hill
A stream at foot, must be there still
Rocks to climb, from an old mining tip
Covered well, fill bucket don't slip
Trees to climb, easy, well known
Trunks some bent, very old grown
Raspberries in sugar, birds' eggs in pan
Branches pulled down, mold wall, no draught.
What more do you want, to camp Sat'day night
Bradwell wood, adventure, place just right
Lads together, such a place of delight
To countless kids, that wood was the place
When they dreamed away childhood
'Twas free all they had,
Sunday, strolling folks, so peaceful
Everything so living, enjoyed by all
Tasted the air, enjoyed as a right
Right at the top, a dug out dell
Clay dug for pots, or so it was said
On the golf links of today
An old ruin stood, and story well known
A pipe of clay led to the wood
Buried and used as a phone,
Somewhere there is a family or two
Whose folk have no need to work
Grandad and his mates saw the way
To blast away that bit of heaven
And make some bricks, an eyesore was left
Makes me sick, who is left to remember
Countless kids, derived of good play
I hate the man who took it away
My dad came home from work that way
Walked up the slope every day
Once trapped in there, much heavy rain
About ten little ones same age as me
Quite a do in our street, kids all gone

H came back with rubber macks
Had seen where we would be
Pitch dark, he pushed in his head
I never forgot, like a visit from God
Come on let's go home, is all he said
Bradder Wood, it's sure gone for good
The bricks for those houses
Poor exchange for our wood.

H Cotterill

CONNIE

She walks with a frame
and never complains
her hearing is not so good
but she manages well
the pension only pays the bills
and some days maybe not.

The meals may not be fancy
but they are good and filling
and keep her warm in the cold
for this winter's a hard one.

The day centre takes her out
a break from these four walls
and a chance to talk
to someone besides herself.

She puts up with a lot
has done since her husband died
but life could be worse
and the television is on.

All in all and by and large
she bears up rather well.

Richard Wallbank

GREY DAY

The fog came down, a thick grey blanket
Closing in all sights and sounds.
The smallest noise made eerie echoes
That were swallowed by the ground.

It swirled around the plants and pathways
Clinging to the tops of trees
Seeping in through nooks and crannies
'Til the house began to freeze.

We threw more fuel on the fire.
'Make a blaze-drive out of the fog'.
Still the vapour crept in with us
Not banished by the burning log.

The house was quiet, all were abed
Deep hidden from the murky mist.
When morning came, the sun arose
And cleared away each lingering wisp.

Margaret Boniface

DECORATING IN BED

Thinking of decorating
Starting in the hall,
I could have it done
But start upon which wall?

I'm thinking of having
Maybe grey and a dark red,
Oh! It's alright dreaming
It's all done in my head.

No! Next week definitely
I will go ahead,
I've just to buy the paper
Once I get out of bed.

L Atherton

SPRING

What are the lambs doing?
Jumping, skipping towards one another
Nuzzling next to their sleepy mother
That's what the lambs are doing.

What are the flowers doing?
They creep through the ground towards the warm sun
Their buds are uncurling one by one
That's what the flowers are doing.

What are the birds doing?
They're singing sweet songs in the early morn
Finding twigs for their nests from the first light of dawn
That's what the birds are doing.

What are the trees doing?
No more bare branches, no brown leaves to fall
Green buds with pink blossom bring joy to us all
That's what the trees are doing.

What is it all about?
A magical carpet of colour appears
People smile and are happy this time of the year
It's spring -
That's what it's all about!

Patricia Jones

FATE

Fate, the lady with atom-bomb shoes
Comes marching our way once more,
Sees the opportunity for chaos
And stirs it just to be sure.

She saw the perfect opportunity
And placed temptation in my way,
Which probably explains the terrible state
My emotions are in today.

Right out of the blue she sent you
To tell me the secrets you'd kept,
Causing feelings lying dormant for aeons
To spring up where they'd slept.

My only regret is that it's taken so long.
Years have passed us by.
Why didn't you tell me way back then?
How could the time not be right?

I wish I knew how to absorb it,
This sudden shock, my awakening.
I've a feeling she has a plan to unveil soon,
Our day of reckoning.

This silly game's been played too long.
My sense of humour wanes.
As Fate raises her arms in triumph
She knows she's got us again . . .

G Mills

THE WAITRESS

Watching her move swiftly between customers,
she wipes the table clean.
'He's leaving me,' she says,
slamming the sugar bowl down.
'That's my second man,
the other one only lasted seven years too.'
I sip my coffee.
'He had the cheek to call me 'Chunky',
him with his beer-swilling gut
he says is muscle.
Do you think I'm chunky?'
'No,' I say to be polite.
Again I sip my coffee, I watch.
She seems obsessed with self-image,
faffing with her hair,
replacing hairpins
falling from unkempt hair.
She straightens her seamed stockings
before wiping hands down apron front.
She is not a pretty sight, this overweight being.
Wearing clothes for the slimmer figure
obesity shows through her nylon blouse,
along with dampness under arm.
Now as she half turns, I catch her cramming the remains
of cake, leaving a cream-covered mouth,
swiftly she wipes away the evidence.
As I finish my coffee, 'Chunky' reappears,
'Sad, init?' she says, emerging from behind the counter.
'I don't know what he expects of me
working in this bakery cake shop . . .'

B Pritchard

PAST FRIENDS

Where did you go
From out our lives?
I think of you so often
Remembering the old days
That now have drifted by.
Do you think the same -
Or did you die?
We lived amongst the chimney stacks
Pointing to the sky.
Happy with our lot -
Everyone our friend, passing by
To daily toil for pennies few.
Do you remember me as I do you.
We danced down the road
The New Year bells were ringing.
No drugs were needed those days
We were high just on our singing.
The years they parted all of us.
We moved to different places.
Now memories bring to mind -
Our crowd, others too. Lots of faces.
Where are they all now?
Living, sometimes thinking as I.
        Or did they die?

Marnie Connley

SUBMISSIONS INVITED
SOMETHING FOR EVERYONE

POETRY NOW '99 - Any subject,
any style, any time.

WOMENSWORDS '99 - Strictly women,
have your say the female way!

STRONGWORDS '99 - Warning!
Age restriction, must be between 16-24,
opinionated and have strong views.
(Not for the faint-hearted)

All poems no longer than 30 lines.
Always welcome! No fee!
Cash Prizes to be won!

Mark your envelope (eg *Poetry Now*) *'99*
Send to:
Forward Press Ltd
Remus House, Coltsfoot Drive,
Woodston,
Peterborough, PE2 9JX

**OVER £10,000 POETRY PRIZES
TO BE WON!**

Judging will take place in October 1999